Du R

8/24/95

Fool Hen Blues

Other Books by E. Donnall Thomas, Jr.

Longbows in the Far North

Whitefish Can't Jump

Longbow Country

Dream Fish and Road Trips

Fool Hen Blues

Retrievers & Shotguns,
and the Birds of the American West

by
E. Donnall Thomas, Jr.

Illustrated by
Christopher Smith

To Nick and Jenny

Published by Wilderness Adventures Press™
P.O. Box 1410
Bozeman, MT 59771

10 9 8 7 6 5 4 3 2 1

Printed in the United States of America

Library of Congress Catalog Card Number: 95-60556

Trade Edition ISBN 1-885106-14-9
Limited Edition of 250 ISBN 1-885106-15-7

Acknowledgements

Several of these pieces have appeared before, in *Shooting Sportsman, Game Journal, Gray's Sporting Journal,* and *Game and Gun.* I appreciate the opportunity to rework the material for inclusion in this volume.

I would like to express my appreciation to a number of writers and editors who have encouraged me to write about the wingshooting life in my own way over the years. This list includes John Barsness, Steve Bodio, Bill Buckley, Eileen Clarke, David Foster, John Hewitt, Angela Smith, Ralph Stuart, and David Wonderlich.

Special thanks go to Steve Smith and Chuck and Blanche Johnson, whose support and enthusiasm have been critical to the success of this project from beginning to end.

Finally, I would like to express my gratitude to the farmers and ranchers of eastern Montana. Without the benefit of their hospitality, I might have had to grow up after all.

I take SPACE to be the central fact to man born in America...I spell it large because it comes large here.

Charles Olson, *Call Me Ishmael*

Table of Contents

Preface

Two themes weave their way through this collection, helping to define its direction and to distinguish it from other personal reminiscences about the wingshooting life.

The first is a matter of venue. All these pieces describe gunning in the American West. This emphasis is largely a reflection of personal experience. My family moved from upstate New York to the Seattle area when I was fifteen and with occasional exceptions driven by educational needs, I have lived in Washington, Alaska, and Montana ever since.

My own experiences with the shotgun may be grounded in coulees and tundra, but the traditions of American wingshooting certainly are not. Our predecessors had generations of experience with grouse, quail, woodcock, and the waterfowl of the Eastern Flyway before anyone out here could stop worrying about day-to-day survival long enough to consider the notion of birds as sport. The art and literature of wingshooting still reflect this accident of history by tending to ignore what goes on out west. Those of us who live here know better.

The second theme is even more of an orphan. In large measure, this collection is a tribute to the versatile retriever. The Lab's credentials in the duck blind are obvious, but more and more of us are asking more and more of our retrievers in the field. In fact, these dogs can be used and enjoyed in the pursuit of almost anything, a concept that is addressed directly in several chapters of this book and indirectly in all the rest.

Celebrating these abilities in print is the least I could do on behalf of all the dogs who have done so much for me.

Pheasants on the Edge

Game is a phenomenon of edges.
—Aldo Leopold

From my hard-earned purchase on the coulee's sidewall, I can peer down into the brush along its narrow bottom, a dense tangle of buffalo berry, thorn apple, wild roses, snakes, coyotes, and—we hope—ring-necked pheasants. The first indication that this high plains version of the Bataan Death March is about to turn into a bird shoot comes, as usual, from one of the dogs. Down there in the guts of the cover, Sky is suddenly focused, nose down, tail alert. His once random enthusiasm has acquired a sense of direction as he works his way toward the apex of the draw some hundred yards away.

"Birds ahead," I call to Ray, who is scrambling along the opposite side of the coulee.

"The Chessies are on, too!" he calls back, and indeed I can now see his dogs paralleling mine in the brush. We both know what is going to happen next. The thing is to be there when it does.

There is no reason now to look for birds or even to follow the course of the dogs. For the next few minutes, our bird hunt is pure aerobics and little else. The view is more scenic than the inside of a typical gym, but the burn in the thighs feels just like the real thing. The plains are a fascinating place and I can spend hours here poking around in search of arrowheads and antler drops and whatnot, but anyone who chooses a time like this to stop and smell the roses might as well leave the shotgun in the truck, because he isn't going to shoot any pheasants.

Lungs straining, I finally crest the lip of the coulee. A golden stubble field stretches away toward the far horizon in contrast to the rugged terrain we have just climbed through. Now the land feels civilized suddenly, its contours uniform and gentle. Here lie the remains of the season's wheat harvest, the stuff that drives the local economy and makes it possible for all of us to survive out here on the prairie—me, my friends, the dogs, and the game. Of more immediate interest, the shallow sea of stubble means that whatever has been running through the brush ahead of the dogs is about to exhaust its cover.

Here on top, the coulee splits into four fingers that claw at the edge of the field like an angry predator. We know the lay of the land here, just as we know the shape of a hundred similar coulees scattered around the county. What we don't know, of course, is just which fingers the birds will use as their final route of escape.

I have a choice to make and judging by the tempo of the dogs' tails in the cover below, I had better make it quickly. One possibility is to split the difference between the two nearest strips of cover. This tactic will double my chances for a shot at something, but the shot is likely to be near the limit of my range. I don't like long shots at pheasants. Determined to do this right or not at all, I gauge the wind, the mood of the dogs, and the phase of the moon and then station myself right at the edge of the nearest finger where the brush surrenders to the world of internal combustion engines at last.

Across the draw, Ray has made a similar calculation. The bark of his deadly 28-gauge announces that he has read the tea leaves correctly. A second report follows and then he is standing with his gun open, fumbling for shells as his two Chessies circle the field in search of the downed roosters.

Forty yards away, a cacophony of wings erupts from the brush and suddenly roosters are flushing everywhere. All of them, unfortunately, are out of range. Then Sky clears the cover, frantic in his efforts to generate a retrieve. One last bird rises at the edge of the stubble, cackling angrily at the way he has been pushed from his hiding place. Rattled by the dog, the rooster makes a wrong turn in midair and passes directly overhead. I drive the shotgun's muzzle through the outline of the bird and slap the trigger going away and that is that—as final and definitive a conclusion to the day as one could imagine.

Then I have my own double open and my game vest off. When the dog completes the retrieve, I drop the bird inside along with the pair I took from the last patch of cover, and that completes my limit. I reload the shotgun, for there is always a chance of flushing a covey of Huns or sharptails on the way back to the truck, but we will no longer be hunting at the pace pheasants demand.

Now it is time to smell the roses.

My father, the consummate gentleman, is always accusing me of hunting pheasants in less-than-gentlemanly ways.

His own comportment in the field is impeccable despite a hardscrabble upbringing in Depression-era Texas, where game was defined as anything edible that did not obviously belong to someone else, and sport meant bringing food to the table with the least expenditure of valuable ammunition. He went on to develop his bird hunting manners in upstate New York, where he trained bird dogs and shot his over-and-under with uncanny accuracy for years. There, shooting a grouse or woodcock usually meant a controlled situation involving a steady pointer and a certain measure of reserve.

He has never quite gotten used to my own prairie ways. When he visits now (and I note how remarkably these demonstrations of paternal affection coincide with the opening day of something), he always studies my mud-spattered truck and kennel full of broad-shouldered retrievers with obvious misgiving. And before the visit is through, he will quietly suggest that my clamorous, sweaty, fast-paced pheasant hunting methods are uncouth, just as he will let me know that he will be back to do it again next year.

My father is right, of course. I do not hunt ring-necked pheasants in a gentlemanly fashion. That is because I do not regard the ring-necked pheasant as a gentleman.

It's not that I don't admire or respect the bird. It would be impossible to spend the amount of time I have spent hunting pheasants unless I did. The fact is that wild roosters can be audacious, cunning, brazen, tenacious, and sly, and they certainly feel no compunction to play by anyone else's rules. They will run relentlessly, hold with nerves of steel, kamikaze your head, crawl into the most devilish recesses of the cover, and finally scare the hell out of you by erupting skyward at your feet in a ground zero burst of noise and color. They will torment your undeserving dog by running in circles and burrowing into layers of thorns, and when all of your tricks have failed, they will not be above spurring your canine friend without mercy at the end of a hard-earned retrieve.

Pheasants are never really yours until they are in the oven. I have had roosters escape from my hand, my game vest, and the back of my truck. Above all else, the wild ringneck is a bird that demands tenacity in its pursuit.

These are birds to hunt all right, but not necessarily according to the Queensbury Rules. I prefer to take the chase right to them on their own terms, in the heart of the sticker bushes, with a gun that shoots where I point it and a dog more intent on outwitting pheasants than fulfilling someone else's definition of style.

Sorry, Dad.

The other day I was sitting in a blind awaiting the company of a thousand mallards who had chosen to have breakfast somewhere else. My mind wandered as it often does under such circumstances, and I began to imagine a cocktail party conversation with one of those self-appointed defenders of wildlife who have become the main reason I seldom go to real parties anymore. Our imaginary dialogue went something like this:

The Defender (modestly belligerent): "Just imagine how many pheasants there would be here if it weren't for bloodthirsty savages like you!"

Your Correspondent (his own gorge rising): "No problem, retriever-breath! There wouldn't be any!"

And this is as true as any opinions expressed in this sort of exchange are ever likely to be. The ring-necked pheasant has become such a fixture in outdoor America that it is sometimes easy to forget how it got here and what allowed it to thrive once it did. The fact is that the presence of wild pheasants in America is the direct result of the efforts of two kinds of Americans: hunters and farmers.

Ring-necked pheasants are clearly depicted in Chinese drawings three thousand years old. Early Greek explorers introduced a closely related species, the black-necked pheasant, to eastern Europe from the Caucasus before the birth of Christ. The blackneck eventually rode the wave of the Roman conquest throughout Europe, where it became widely valued for its appeal in the field and on the table.

The first attempts to introduce pheasants to the New World involved sporadic introductions of blacknecks along the east coast in the late 1700s. These efforts failed because the boreal habitat there suited the species poorly. American upland gunners had to be content with native grouse and quail for most of the next century. Then in 1881, Owen Denny, American Consul to Shanghai, shanghaied a crate of true Chinese ringnecks and shipped them across the Pacific to his brother's farm in the Willamette Valley. Ten years later, there were enough wild pheasants for

Oregon to hold its first open season. Observers estimated that fifty thousand birds were harvested on opening day. Autumn in the West has never been the same.

The relationship of pheasants to agriculture has an equally rich historical background. Marco Polo reported that the Kublai Khan maintained uncut fields of grain just for the benefit of his pheasants. One can imagine that the Great Khan had means of dealing with poachers that modern game wardens can only view with envy.

Next to Judge Denny's original inspiration, the most formative event in the history of American pheasant hunting took place in Sarajevo prior to the First World War. To be honest, I can't remember who shot whom, probably because I skipped that part of history class to go hunting. At the time the War to End All Wars began, Russia was the world's largest exporter of wheat. Russia, as those who studied history at less inconvenient times of the year will recall, has always suffered from a shortage of warmwater ports. When Turkey blockaded the Dardenelles, the rest of the world suddenly found itself trying to make sandwiches without any bread. Subsequent market pressures lead to a flurry of agricultural activity on the American plains, ironically aided by the development of hardy strains of wheat from Russian stock. Farm equipment of the day was tough enough to till the prairie but not tough enough to tear through the brush. The result was just the sort of edges that Aldo Leopold had in mind.

Food and cover, food and cover—a recurring theme in wildlife biology that is absolutely central to the success of the pheasant here on the high plains. Cover is not a critical problem on the prairie in its native state, which in fact offers habitat remarkably similar to the pheasant's original haunts on the Old World steppe. Food is a more complicated matter. As the Mongol emperor observed seven centuries ago, pheasants do best with lots of it, especially when it is concentrated conveniently near their hiding places.

Ecological purists will protest that the successful introduction of an exotic species such as the pheasant must come at the expense of something else. They are correct, but only if the ecosystem is in a steady state. This one clearly is not. All that wheat is a nutritional bounty for many species. Problems arise when agricultural practices encroach upon critical escape habitat, at which point all those amber waves of grain stop doing wildlife any good. Such considerations explain why I find the truest expression of pheasant habitat and pheasant hunting here on the high plains where mountains spill down onto the prairie and rugged breaks and coulees defy the plow at the very edge of the great American bread basket.

This is game country all right, the sort of habitat that produces wild hunts for wild birds in wild terrain. The birds' presence and the enjoyment I derive from them are precisely linked to the country's basic incivility. There will be no organized drives across corn fields here, no leisurely strolls down well-defined fence rows. After generations of selective pressure from coyotes, raptors, and guys like me, these pheasants have developed traits as wild as the cover they inhabit, and one must hunt them accordingly.

Our local methods are the product of years of experience hunting these birds on a regular basis. This approach is challenging, effective, and capable of driving our visitors crazy, especially those who come with the notion that bird hunting should reflect some underlying sense of social order. There are rules, of course, involving gun safety, points of law, and sportsmanship. There is even a complex form of etiquette among the two or three people I hunt with regularly, although this would be difficult to explain to an outsider. These principles are often served best when they are left unstated. Should you find yourself hunting with someone who needs to be told such things, it would usually be best for all concerned if he or she went back to a more controlled environment to learn the basics.

The underlying theory upon which all this strategy is based is that wild pheasants will run until they are forced to do something else. Getting one airborne generally requires three things: a limiting terrain feature, a determined dog, and a mistake on the part of the pheasant. And making the rise take place where you can do something about it requires familiarity with the cover, a feel for pheasant behavior, intuitive communication with the dog, and enthusiasm for vigorous exercise. I seldom realize how complex all this can get until I watch a visitor try to do it, especially if the visitor is an otherwise experienced bird hunter. Newcomers to the game often wind up at the wrong place at the wrong time and it is hard to tell them how to do otherwise. No wonder my father arrives with all those misgivings.

My own choice of shotguns is simple, stubborn, and perhaps surprising to those unfamiliar with western bird hunting. While enjoying a sentimental attachment to my vintage Parker, I come down on the short-barreled, improved cylinder side of the argument whenever I want to put some serious pheasant on the table. As noted, regular hunting partner Ray Stalmaster shoots a 28-gauge side-by-side, a choice of weapons many would regard as inadequate for open country pheasant hunting. Suffice it to say that he shoots it well, knows his range, and handles a pair of Chessies that cover the prairie like vacuum cleaners. To full-choke, smoke-and-thunder diehards I would only say that if birds are out of range, you shouldn't shoot at them with anything, and we don't. Adherence to this principle makes unrecovered pheasants rare, solemn events on our hunts.

While I still have great respect for the aesthetics of the pointing breeds, my kennel contains nothing but retrievers nowadays, and not simply because I like them. It is a sad fact that the skills a flushing retriever can bring to bear on this kind of hunting go largely unrecognized. The ability of these dogs is difficult to appreciate, measure, or represent in any artistic medium. There is really no way to train a dog to do this except to do it, although I will discuss my own approach to training flushing retrievers in a later chapter. The problem is that the tricks required to flush a running pheasant in the right place at the right time cannot be taught in the backyard. Even here, in the heart of bird country, it generally takes four or five seasons for a dog to learn the trade well, and then it is only a matter of time until all those hard miles and long days begin to take their physical toll. But when you have established a unique, personal rapport with a pheasant hunting Lab based on years of shared experience in the field, and each of you knows what the other is going to do without benefit of whistles and commands, then the shot and the retrieve and the quiet moment of appreciation at the end become their own reward, even if no one understands except another prairie pheasant hunter.

It is still possible to become acquainted with pheasant country the old fashioned way even if you don't live here. My advice? Take some time out of your busy life and knock on some farmhouse doors. It will do you good to get to know the people who feed the game, not to mention yourself and your family. Such relationships can become as rewarding a part of the hunt as the shooting itself. If you plan to hunt here, you really should know something of farmbelt economics and its inequities. You will have people tell you that you cannot hunt, of course, and you will hear the usual excuses—how the foxes ate all the birds this spring (this while five dozen pheasants scurry around the barnyard in front of you), and how they are saving the place for their non-existent in-laws who are coming down next week. You will also hear about the truckload of guys who came out opening day and shot the place up and left the gates open and scattered beer cans all over the place, and now there by-God isn't going to be any more hunting for the rest of the year—but you need to hear this too, and the tone of righteous anger never really comes through in translation.

After a few days of this you will be ready to tell me that I am a lucky guy because I have managed to live my life in remote places where the hunting is good and the pheasants are wild and none of this seems to be accessible to outsiders. I will then tell you that it really isn't luck at all, that anyone can do it with a proper ordering of their priorities. Then you will say that I have got to be kidding, that no responsible person would really forsake career and money and cultural amenities just to live in places where there are wild pheasants.

And I will say: Wanna bet?

Late Season

Nothing friendly waits outside my window anymore. The mixed flocks of puddle ducks are gone and the marshes and potholes that bred them stand frozen and silent, immobilized by winter's embrace. Deer season is over and the Huns hanging in the barn will be the year's final upland bird harvest. All the dogs want inside, and the nights have been so cold that I have relented to even the most ill-mannered of the lot. At times like this, it is an easy matter to resign oneself to oiling guns and tying flies and dreaming of bonefish flats in faraway, unaffordable places. If it weren't for the creek, I'd probably be doing just that myself.

The creek that defines our valley is a true spring creek, and it runs smooth and even all year long no matter what the weather. An old rancher told me that he once saw it frozen from bank to bank below town, but in my own two decades here I've never seen ice do anything more than form a delicate trim along the creek's edges. Winter just can't seem to get a hold on its laughing water, as if it enjoys some kind of immunity from the cold. The creek's open flow is guaranteed good down to thirty below, and the security of its presence is what keeps the mallards here in the valley even when every pond and reservoir in the county is frozen hard enough to drive a truck across.

There isn't much variety during our late season. Occasionally, one of us will drop a lonely goldeneye or even a confused goose, but for practical purposes this is a mallards-only club, featuring plump, full-feathered birds so full of grain that their crops crunch like bean bags when the dog delivers them to your hand. Roast a brace of greenheads like these and serve them in good company, and they will taste like they were created for no purpose other than to be eaten with enthusiasm.

The paradox of the ducks' late season affinity for the creek is their loathing for small, confining waters. They feel vulnerable there, and not without reason. When weather conditions permit, they will predictably scatter to whatever water is open, leaving the creek all but barren. Let the casual water freeze and back they will come, as if under contract. During the late season, nasty weather seems to be central to the pursuit of ducks, just as snow is central to the pursuit of elk and rain is central to the pursuit of steelhead. As is usually the case with waterfowling, the more reasonable the weather out there, the less reason to be outdoors enjoying it.

While an experienced gunner with local knowledge can put a duck dinner on the table almost any day during the late season, quality shooting is absolutely temperature dependent. Above freezing, one is essentially reduced to subsistence hunting, complete with belly crawls, two man end-arounds, and other low-rent jump shooting tactics (not to imply that I haven't done my share of that sort of thing). When the mercury begins the day between zero and freezing, it becomes reasonable to expect productive shooting over decoys. And when the thermometer bottoms out and the truck won't start without a block heater and any suggestion of a breeze sends the chill factor slicing right through the last layer of your dignity, you can anticipate a duck hunt the likes of which you may never experience anywhere else.

The rolling country here on the plains makes the altitude deceptive. These are the headwaters of the Missouri after all, and it's downhill for a long way to the Gulf of Mexico. If you were to land an airplane in my alfalfa field, its altimeter would read just under five thousand feet as it rolled to a stop. All this means that our hunting takes place in mountain air despite the apparent lack of mountainous terrain. When a serious arctic high moves down from the north as one did earlier this week, nothing but rarefied vapor stands between human observers and the stars. They glimmer down upon us now with almost unnatural intensity even in the face of the dull glow of light from the east: the Dippers, Cassiopeia, and finally Orion and the Dog Star, personal favorites for obvious reasons. You have never really seen the stars until you have seen them from the high plains at twenty below zero.

The snow is so cold and dry that it squeaks beneath our boots as we walk. Crossing barbed wire fences in the dark is a tricky proposition when it's this cold, and it's asking a lot of a pair of chest waders to expect them to survive an entire season of such abuse. I certainly hope this one has. Up ahead, a layer of ice fog hangs above the creek like a shroud, and as it closes over our heads the stars disappear from sight completely. We can't see just where we are going, but the path to the pool is fixed by repetition. I have come here too often to lose my bearings, no matter what the visibility.

As dawn begins to break, the light level rises slowly inside the envelope of fog to reveal a fantastic display of ice crystals on the brush lining the creek bank. Moisture from the creek's warm surface has risen and condensed higher and higher up on the branches throughout the night, creating a vast network of filaments ready to sparkle in the morning sun. Even the dog seems transfixed by the sight, as if he cannot quite get his bearings. When I close my eyes and listen to the water flow, I can imagine for a moment that I have brought a fly rod instead of a shotgun. This is a measure of the creek's indifference to the seasons. How little time has passed since I stood right in that riffle wearing nothing more than worn-out running shoes and cut-off jeans and worked a nymph upstream into the dying embers of the evening. Now it is hard to imagine trout suspended there beneath the cold, black surface of the creek. Somehow though, there is enough consistency in this place to accommodate ice crystals and summer sunsets alike. I suspect the common denominator is the sound the water makes. No wonder I always find that sound worth listening to.

Mornings like this make me wonder why we have never discovered how to train our dogs to set out decoys for us. In the meanwhile, one of us will just have to do it. I lean my double against the downed cottonwood that passes for a blind and gingerly wade forward.

There will be no elaborate decoy spread this morning, partly because of the unpleasantness of dealing with them in the cold and partly because the decoys themselves are all but unnecessary. A half-dozen will suffice, which is about as many as the pool can accommodate and at least three more than my freezing fingers want to handle. By ten o'clock on a morning like this, every bend in the creek is likely to be stuffed with mallards, and the object now is simply to make this one no more unattractive than any other.

Inside our makeshift blind, the first real light of day plays across Sky's features and turns his coat a rich, luminous yellow. His breath has condensed upon his muzzle, where the cold has turned the moisture into a halo of silver that quivers in short bursts as he shivers. I cannot get over how contented he looks in spite of it all. Bred for generations just to be here, he is at the apogee of his purpose as a Labrador retriever, and it just doesn't get any better than that.

The same cannot be said of us. We both know that the first rule of duck blind conduct is to keep still. Now as sunlight filters through the

fog and ice begins to accumulate upon the leading edges of the decoys tacking back and forth in the current, this simple principle becomes impossible to obey. At first it is just fidgeting, a shuffling of the feet and the random motion of chilled hands inside our pockets. Then our arms begin to swing and finally we are pacing up and down the bank in a mindless effort to stay warm. Finally, I wonder aloud if we will make the national news for this one. It is easy to imagine the headline blaring from the supermarket tabloids: "Demented Hunters Freeze to Death One Hundred Yards from Safety!"

Enduring misery courtesy of the weather is a theme common to a number of wonderful outdoor sports, of which winter steelhead fishing and bowhunting rutting whitetails are prime examples. This morning's experience along the creek can rival any of them. It is so cold that my teeth hurt. The steam rising from the water presses in against the flesh like toxic vapor, biting at everything it touches. The point of this has broad implications for all outdoor sports: Nature doesn't care whether you're having a good time out there or not. Human happiness is of no intrinsic consequence to anyone or anything except humans. If you want to enjoy yourself in the field, you will have to adjust your frame of reference and convince your skeptical body that flirting with hypothermia is not necessarily any reason to stop having a good time.

And then the ducks appear to affirm our patience after all. At first they are nothing but noises, an arrhythmic series of whistles and tears in the air overhead accompanied by the warm feeding chuckle of contented mallards. Suddenly, the sky above us is full of ducks. Today it doesn't matter whether they like the creek or not, for the weather has eliminated the luxury of choice. There is nothing left for them to do but to come in side-slipping and back-peddling as they jockey for position in the crowded airspace above the creek.

We reject several marginal pass shooting opportunities and then a dozen mallards are suddenly suspended over the decoys. Iridescent green heads crane forward and orange feet extend to ease the birds' arrival upon the water. Then one of them flares and they all strain noisily back toward the sky. In an instant of calculation, we mentally separate drakes from hens and stand and swing, and after two barrels apiece, four birds are bobbing downstream on the relentless current. It is time for the dog at last.

Late season dog work is an art in its own right. The heroic potential of retrievers in cold water is obvious, but cold is only part of the challenge. The concept of moving water is foreign to retriever instincts and much of their traditional education. After all, we spend great effort teaching our dogs to mark and hunt tenaciously where the bird falls. Late season dog work almost always takes place over flowing water, where simple physics assure that the traditional approach to getting dogs and dead ducks in the same place won't work. I have watched more than one experienced retriever spend his first morning on the creek treading water in frustration while his quarry floated downstream and out of his life. It is often the best trained visiting dogs that turn in the most pathetic performances here.

And so in this part of the country, we train our dogs in all sorts of heretical ways. They are introduced to moving water as puppies and taught the concept of "downstream" from the time they first start to retrieve. They learn to negotiate sweepers and tricky currents under controlled conditions, during the summer, when we can be in the water to help them. And with apologies to the strict traditionalists in the crowd, we encourage them to run the banks. With a handful of dead mallards floating downstream, knowing the shortest way to the ducks may mean the difference between retrieves and losses. These compromises lead to their own style of dog work at which purists are free to scoff, but the retrieve itself is the final measure of accomplishment in the field.

Skykomish is out of the blocks at once. With multiple birds down in moving water, it is usually a mistake to over-control the dog. Sky is a veteran, and as long as he is headed in the right direction, it is best to let him work things out for himself without interrupting the flow of events with whistles and unnecessary commands. Two of the downed drakes are circling lazily in an eddy, and he has both of them accounted for in less time than it takes to tell about it. The third has hung up in a pile of beaver workings fifty yards downstream from the decoys, where the dog negotiates the current easily and makes the retrieve look routine.

Stone dead, the fourth duck has bobbed away out of sight. I sit the dog against my knee and send him downstream along the bank. A hundred yards away, he hits the water and works his way back upstream toward us. When he arrives, the last duck is in his mouth. A modest vindication of his unorthodox upbringing, this retrieve is one of those accomplishments that is easier to enjoy than it is to teach, or even to explain. Finally, the last flights of the morning are straggling in from the stubble fields. We could shoot a few more ducks, and in fact we do, but that is scarcely the point. Our goals this morning were to obtain the makings of a duck dinner, to work the dog, and to bear witness to a phenomenon. By returning to the creek despite their mistrust of it, the ducks have fulfilled a promise to those of us willing to get out of bed and be there waiting for them.

The events of the morning cannot be framed in terms of bag limits or challenge to the gun. Dropping mallards over decoys at close range is to wingshooting what the sword is to the bullfight—a necessary conclusion, but scarcely the heart of the matter. It is the intimacy of all those birds brought together by natural circumstance and the elegance of their arrival upon the creek that drew us here, and that is just as surely what will draw us back again.

Sunlight is dancing on the snow by the time we pack up to leave, creating an illusion of warmth that the thermometer does not confirm. Perhaps it is the mood rather than the temperature that has risen, driven by the shooting, the good dog work, and the feel of birds in the game bag. Now the promise of more winter to come seems attenuated somehow, despite the layers of ice along the water's edge and the cold, windswept leads of snow stretching away from the creek in all directions. We are ready for the rest of the schedule. Our morning on the creek has shown us the way. That may finally be what the best of the outdoors has to offer us—a means of reckoning with the rest.

Asking a Friend

During the cross country jumping phase of the 1992 Badminton horse trials, several top-level event horses sustained lethal injuries on the field. This sad footnote in the annals of international equestrian affairs doesn't seem to have much to do with wingshooting. I admit that the only reason I know anything about the matter is that my wife at the time was an event ride, and we discussed many of the issues that these mishaps raised in riding circles, which in fact may be of more significance to hunters than one might imagine.

After this unfortunate horse trial, equestrian sports enjoyed, if that is the word, some unwelcome scrutiny from a familiar group of characters— the animal rights crowd. This should have come as no surprise, since the anti-hunting movement can trace its own historical origins to the fox hunting traditions of the British Isles. Now that no one actually kills foxes during fox hunts anymore, the animal rightists have shifted their attention to the next available target—the horses themselves.

Anyone familiar with the standards of care for competitive jumping horses (and there is no one so familiar with those standards as the former spouse of a serious rider) may have difficulty imagining anyone taking such charges seriously. Around our place, horses certainly enjoyed better care than I did. Of course, in my opinion, rationality has never been a prominent feature of the animal rights agenda. Defenders asserted that the will to compete is part of the top-level event horse's character. Critics charged that this is only because such qualities had been put there. I followed this story with mounting fascination, because it was starting to sound very much like so many discussions I have had over the years about hunting dogs. Which is why I think dead horses may be significant to those of us who spend our autumns in the field with dog and gun.

We do ask a lot of our dogs, and in the spirit of intellectual honesty, it seems worth asking whether we sometimes ask more than we should.

One November day a number of years ago I was bouncing along at the wheel of my pickup with regular hunting partner, Ray Stalmaster, and Joe Kelly, an out-of-state friend. Ray and I had spent the day helping our visitor fill a deer tag, and a good buck now lay in the back of the truck along with a few incidental Huns, sage hens, and Sky, my Lab, who always went along no matter what we happened to be hunting.

The prairie had the steely look that it often acquires in November, as if it were ready to reach out and bite us. There was no color in the monotonous landscape of snow and rock and sage. It was late in the season and most of the casual water had frozen. Although we weren't equipped for waterfowling in any formal sense of the term, I had a sudden urge to send Joe home with a duck dinner that evening. As we crossed the head of a draw that contained a large stock pond in its lower reaches, I stopped and sent Ray up the bank to see if it contained any open water with jumpable ducks. He scooted back down a moment later and assured us that there were at least twenty mallards tucked in behind the earthen dam in the lee of the wind.

We circled around the coulee, climbed out of the truck, and loaded our bird guns with the heaviest shells we could find. (This event took place in the days before steel shot, for which we should all feel grateful.) Finally, we hiked up the draw to the dam. There we coordinated our final approach perfectly and crested the top of the dam together to discover an intelligence blunder worthy of Custer's Last Stand: the twenty mallards had somehow become two hundred geese, which now took to the air in a cacophony of noise and wings barely a dozen yards in front of our faces.

Of course I prefer to shoot my geese over decoys like a gentleman, but, well, there they were. After the first collective gasp of disbelief, each of us settled down to the business of picking targets from the flock. We were all shooting doubles and we immediately had six geese down in the patch of open water behind the dam. Three were stone dead, but the rest were heading in different directions as fast as they could swim.

At my command, the dog had remained behind in the sagebrush as we climbed up the back side of the dam, but he was at my side by the time the shooting stopped. He quickly collected the three easy marks, and then I sent him around the perimeter of the pond in the direction taken by the first of the cripples. It took him five minutes to run the goose down in the sagebrush. We then repeated the process on the other side of the pond, and we soon had the fifth bird in hand.

The last goose had set its wings and sailed far out onto the ice beyond the open water. By the time we collected the first five birds, it was all the way out in the middle of the frozen pond, where it now rested at least two hundred yards from the nearest shore. We picked up our guns and walked the edge of the pond to the point nearest the goose. After studying the situation again, I sat Sky down and scratched his ears.

As we looked at the distant black outline of the goose so far away across the windswept sheet of ice, it suddenly seemed that the dog had been born in order to make this retrieve and no other. Years of training and work and companionship had come down to this. I gave him the line and sent him.

"What are you going to do if he falls through the ice?" Ray asked.

"Go out and get him," I replied without hesitation.

"And who is going to go out there and get you?" Ray wondered.

"You are," I said with equal conviction. What are hunting partners for, anyway?

The dog proceeded deliberately across the ice. It was not that he lacked determination. He was just cautious, and he already had five heavy retrieves under his belt. Sixty yards out, he realized that he hadn't found anything worth finding, so he sat down and looked back at me for instructions.

"You can call this off," Ray said. It was neither a request nor a suggestion. He was simply trying to offer the possibility of a graceful retreat from what was rapidly becoming a difficult situation. That was precisely when I realized that I couldn't call it off, not with the goose sitting there in plain sight. We had assumed certain responsibilities when we walked over the top of the dam with shotguns in our hands, and I had assumed another set of responsibilities when I lined the dog out and sent him on the retrieve. These are not the sort of responsibilities hunters take lightly. I raised my arm and signaled the dog to continue farther out once more. Sky trotted dutifully on. He had gone another thirty yards toward the goose when the sound of ice cracking exploded like a pistol shot through the air. The dog hesitated. Nothing about the afternoon seemed comfortable or fun anymore.

My friends looked at me. I recognized an assault by my own worst instincts—stubbornness, pride, and an overriding lack of flexibility. Sky and I made eye contact across a hundred yards of ice, and we held a sort of telepathic discussion about the wisdom of going on with this. He indicated nothing but enthusiasm and I urged him on again.

Although the goose was still nearly a hundred yards farther away across the ice, it stood out plainly against the flat white background, and I could tell by Sky's sudden focal intensity that he had seen the bird at last. We would need no more hand signals. Even so, he proceeded thoughtfully, feeling his way along the surest possible route across the ice. When he finally pounced on the goose, the bird offered no resistance. He held his head high all the way back toward shore as if he understood that the goose in his mouth represented a triumph, at least in the eyes of his nervous audience.

Together on the frozen mud at last, I accepted the bird and handed it to my friends. Then I knelt beside Sky. No one said anything for some time as I stroked his head and dwelt upon my own overwhelming sense of relief. The Lab suddenly looked vulnerable and I thought of the seasons we had shared and how one segment of my own life experience could be defined by the time we had spent together. Time was playing tricks on all of us.

"You know that was the Retrieve of the Year," Ray said finally.

This Retrieve of the Year business had been going on as long as Ray owned Chessies and I owned Labs, which was a long time indeed. What started out as a gentle rivalry between enthusiasts of two different breeds had evolved into a tradition of solemn significance. The rules for awarding the Retrieve of the Year were like the rules for calling fouls in playground basketball—each of us could only make the call on behalf of the other's dog. Once declared, the choice was never disputed. This was an honor, this Retrieve of the Year. I understood that and in a dangerously romantic sense I like to think that the dog did, too. As we toasted the retrieve over a goose dinner that evening, it occurred to me that I would never forget the day's events. And I haven't.

Our impassioned response to that retrieve is the sort of thing that is almost impossible to explain to others unless they share with you a basic set of assumptions: that the world is at all times a potentially volatile place; that life is better lived on the edge than from beneath your covers; that all worthwhile undertakings may entail some degree of risk to yourself and others, including those you love.

This simple dog story could have ended in tragedy rather than triumph. I could have lost the dog through the ice. My family could have lost me. The afternoon could have degenerated into one of those chain reactions of catastrophe like a series of collisions on a snow covered interstate, with all of us becoming a collective reminder of what happens when enthusiasm exceeds common sense.

I believe that the emotion we are trying to come to terms with here is indeed passion, not in the traditional sense of the romance novel, but in the Latin sense, as suggested by the bullfight, in which animals evoke our emotional response through the purity of their own will. One cannot make a bull charge bravely anymore than one can make a dog plunge into icy water or a horse jump over a fence to land upon unseen footing. The will to do such things comes from within. And whether one finds truth or terror in any of these acts may ultimately depend more upon the observer than what is observed. Finally, there can be no passion without danger, and without passion, well...

Let us take the argument to its limit. If my dog had fallen through the ice and died on that retrieve, of what would I be guilty? Cruelty? Betrayal of trust? Let me submit that it would have been more of a betrayal to turn and walk away. The most pathetic sounds ever heard from Labrador retrievers come from those who are denied the opportunity to hunt. That may be the most difficult part of watching a dog outlive his own heart and legs in the winter of his years. In the end, Sky trusted me to take him hunting, and I did.

I wish the horses had not fallen at Badminton. I wish Ray's Chessie had not drowned later that year in an ice-choked river. For that matter, I wish Sky hadn't died peacefully in his sleep the summer after he made the last of several Retrieves of the Year, but there isn't much anyone can do about that, either.

That dog and I were able to hunt together. I asked him to help me and he did, with passion. Both of us lived fuller lives as a consequence. I can take the discussion no further than that.

The rest is silence.

Fool Hen Blues

L et us call the first witness to the stand. It is the second week of
September. I am headed back toward camp, hot, tired, and wryly
amused that the elk have proven themselves smarter than me once again.
My longbow hangs loosely from my left hand as my brain idles in neutral. I am no longer hunting but hiking. Suddenly a flurry of wings carries a dark, gallinaceous bird into a nearby pine tree, and I am a predator
again. My new-found intensity has nothing to do with the romance of
wingshooting, fine shotguns, or bird dogs. All I want out of this
encounter is the brief, exquisite feel of one good arrow and the ingredi-
ents for my dinner.

Acutely aware of my preference for fresh grouse over canned chili, I
keep one eye on the bird and slowly ease an arrow onto the bowstring.
This is not the blunt that I carry for practice but a genuine, lethal broad-
head. I then take three steps to the side in order to make the pine tree
itself a back-stop in case of a miss (perish the thought). My right hand
finds its anchor point at the corner of my mouth and releases. The bird
flinches at the sound of the bow, but does not flush. The arrow thuds
harmlessly into the tree trunk with its fletches vibrating inches from my
quarry's face, just the way Indian arrows used to hit the sides of covered
wagons in the old western movies we all watched as kids. Believe it or
not, I missed indeed. A quiver full of arrows remains, however, and dinner doesn't seem to be going anywhere.

And now, our second witness.

Same mountains, same ridge, three weeks later. I am now equipped
with a 12-gauge double instead of a bow, and one of the Labs frolics at
my side. There is a simple pleasure that comes from walking through
these woods without regard to the wind or the crunch my boots make on
the dry carpet underfoot. I couldn't have moved this casually earlier, but I
am through with elk now and I see the mountains differently. Once again
I am grouse hunting, but this time I am doing it as seriously as I know
how.

"Explode" is an inflated verb in outdoor writing, what with ducks being called upon to do it from potholes, whitetails from patches of buck brush, and rainbows every time they take a fly from the surface of some quiet stream. But as I work my way around a stand of burnished aspens and watch the dog disappear into a tangle of brush, that is exactly what the first blue grouse does and there is just no other way to report the event. It is an assertive sound, this percussion of wings, and one that would demand that you turn and stare even if you had no interest in grouse or their pursuit. I track the wingbeat instinctively and when the bird hurtles across a gap in the trees, I do my best to have the column of six-shot waiting there on schedule. Nothing falls but leaves, however, and I have the over-and-under broken to reload when the second bird flushes and sails away down the mountainside in plain sight.

I will jump a dozen blues on the ridge this morning, manage shots at five, and be damned proud of the three in my game vest when I finally stagger back to the truck after hours of wrestling contour lines. Not one of that dozen will waddle through the woods in front of me or flap mindlessly into a pine tree as I watch. Only by conscious effort can I convince myself that these are the same birds I was killing with arrows less than a month earlier.

And now, members of the jury: Will you identify for the court the *real* blue grouse?

In my part of the world, bird hunting generally means working the prairie for pheasants, sharptails, sage grouse, and Huns. It's a hard premise to argue with, since plains habitat offers a smorgasbord of game, unobstructed shooting, and an opportunity to hunt all day without dying of exhaustion. But there are mountains here as well, and those mountains are home to three species that are usually all but overlooked by serious bird hunters. The West's so-called mountain grouse—Franklin's, ruffs, and blues—are lumped together here in Montana in one derivative category for legal purposes, the idea being that big game hunters can shoot their heads off with rifles more or less indiscriminately while "real" bird hunters are down on the prairie hunting "real" gamebirds in civilized ways. What a shame this benign neglect turns out to be, for at its best, at least one of these species—the blue—ranks among the most challenging and rewarding shotgun quarries in North America.

My personal affection for the blue grouse has deep historical roots, as is often the case in discussions of this sort. Western flora is usually dominated by conifers or prairie grasses depending on the elevation, but there are deciduous trees this side of the Mississippi as well, and they turn brilliant colors in the fall, just as they do in the East. These pockets of aspen and birch are part and parcel of blue grouse cover, and in the fall they remind me of upstate New York, where I was first introduced to the craft of wingshooting more than three decades ago. It is this blue grouse habitat that lets me close my eyes and listen to the dry leaves stirring in the wind and remember our bird dogs and the secret names we gave our favorite patches of cover and my father's careful tutelage in the way of the hunting life. Memory can't do much more for you, and now it is the blue that lets the genie out of the bottle as easily as any gamebird I know.

And there is something of the eastern partridge in the blue itself, at least on its better days. Consider how the wings announce the flush, how the bird appears to tease its way through the cover as it flies, and how the shot feels so utterly correct when all goes well. I love my Huns and sharptails and all the rest, but somehow none of those open country species can make me feel quite the way a good day of blue grouse shooting does.

But then there is that "fool hen" business, so welcome to hungry elk hunters and such a burden to the blue's reputation among those who take their wingshooting seriously. Since I can fall into either category myself depending on the season, my inclination, and the state of my elk tag, I am sensitive to the blue's schizophrenic identity problems and can offer some observations from both perspectives.

Fool hens are different things to different people at different times, and it is impossible to understand the blue's role in this scheme without an overview of western mountain grouse and their sometimes eccentric pursuit.

Franklin's grouse and their northern relatives, the spruce grouse, are the definitive fool hens. Their habit of fluttering up into low-lying branches when disturbed is actually quite adaptive when you consider that overhanging limbs shield them from raptors and an elevation of eight or ten feet is enough to put them beyond the reach of most ground-level predators. Alas for the unfortunate spruce grouse, hungry humans weren't part of the selective pressures that made it what it is today. Their pattern of escape behavior isn't much use in defense from human predators, even those carrying nothing more sophisticated than sticks. When I lived in Alaska, I used to walk the abandoned seismic trails around my home while my Labs tore through the cover on either side. Occasionally, a spruce grouse would hurtle across the opening in front of me before it could perch in a tree, affording something like a grouse shot. You may be assured that this was wingshooting in its most desperate form. Color spruce grouse foolish and leave them for survival fare. Somewhere there's a hungry hunter who is going to need them.

Legions of devoted enthusiasts will be appalled to find the ruffed grouse included in this company at all. The sad fact is that the western version of the ruff just isn't the same bird as its eastern counterpart. I spent enough of my youth in alder thickets and abandoned apple orchards to develop great respect for the ruffed grouse, but the fact is that the species seems to have left its brains behind when it crossed the Great Plains. This is one of the few disappointments to be found when bird hunting the West. Ruffed grouse are actually the dominant gamebird in the timbered coulees around my Montana home, and we shall examine in a later chapter my occasional attempts to turn their presence there into sport. Such acts of contrition notwithstanding, out here the noble ruff is by and large just another flavor of soup. Sorry, boys.

And then there is the blue. Tall, dark, and handsome, the blue is by far the largest of the mountain grouse species. Among American game-birds, only the sage hen and the turkey outweigh it. The blue's range straddles the Continental Divide from northern California to the Yukon. East and west slope versions differ enough so that ornithologists have been known to argue about separating them into two distinct species.

My personal experience with blue grouse west of the Continental Divide is limited. My Alaska years were spent well north of the blue's range. In Alaska's southeast panhandle, however, they are a popular gamebird. They are referred to there as "hooters" because of the male's distinctive spring mating call. Spring grouse hunts in southeast Alaska are both legal and socially acceptable, reflecting the fact that by the time winter draws to a close up north you are ready to do damn near anything. Friends who have survived hooter hunts report that the birds are actually *called*, like turkeys—sort of. It seems that the best hooter call ever devised is an empty beer bottle. A typical spring hooter hunt entails hol-ing up beside a wood stove in a cabin somewhere manufacturing hooter calls by the case while everyone waits for it to stop raining long enough to go hunting. Of course, it never stops raining in southeast Alaska. One imagines that hooter hunting is something of an acquired taste.

I am far more familiar with the east slope version of the blue grouse, technically known as the Richardson subspecies. While this bird can sometimes present fool hen credentials sufficient to satisfy anyone, it can also provide gunning tough enough to challenge the most experienced of wingshots. That is why when the air turns crisp I still find myself forsaking the pleasures of sharptails and elk and heading to the mountains with my shotgun just to hunt blues.

Good blue grouse habitat usually consists of a mixture of pine and deciduous trees broken by creek bottoms and alpine glades. Fall is a marvelous season in the mountain West and you really don't have to do a lot of shooting in order to enjoy yourself there. You will see fresh bear sign if you look. Late mushrooms are at their best and there is no limit on shaggy manes. Elk rubs mark the smaller pines and the edges of the aspen groves, and if you listen you will be as likely to hear a bugle as a grouse's flush.

While most mountain species begin the fall at higher elevations and slowly move lower as winter approaches, blue grouse are almost unique in their habit of performing this annual migration in reverse. Early in the year, I have flushed blues from thorn apple thickets scarcely removed from sharptail cover. But as ice shows up on the ponds in the morning and noisy southbound geese begin to interfere with sleep, blues head higher toward the windswept ridges where they will eventually spend the winter. So where will they be in October when you really want to hunt them? Beats me. If you are having trouble locating birds, park at the end of the road and start hiking uphill until you find them. As you might imagine, it helps to wear good hiking boots and take your most vigorous dog along. And don't forget to pack a lunch.

And speaking of lunch...
I have a complex personal relationship with wild game as table fare. I grew up in a family of hunters and cooks, so most of the animal protein I have consumed over the years has come from something put on the table by myself or my circle of family and friends. I enjoy birds and ducks and venison in the kitchen almost as much as I do in the field and have waged a long campaign to convert reluctant wild game eaters to the cause. With all that said, I still don't regard myself as a meat hunter for complex reasons that would take a long evening around a campfire to articulate clearly.

Nonetheless, there are three species of gamebirds that I would conspire to get onto my table under any biologically defensible circumstances, even if getting them there had nothing to do with bird dogs and shotguns and all the other trappings of sport. I would take these three with bird lime if I had to. I would even go to the store and buy them in little cellophane packages, just because they taste so good. For the record, this culinary elite consists of the blue-winged teal, the mourning dove, and the blue grouse.

If you have made it home with a brace of blues in your game vest, you can fillet the breasts and prepare the meat any way light poultry brings to mind without being disappointed. I would suggest, however, that you simply pluck the birds and roast them whole, basted with the seasoned butter of your choice, and serve along with wild rice, tossed salad, and a good Chardonnay. This minimalist approach showcases the blue's light flavor and tenderness, unrivaled by any other American gamebird. Remember how large they are. They require a bit more time in the oven than other grouse, and unless you are really hungry you can share one with your significant other and not leave the table feeling shorted. Of course, blue grouse hunters always seem to be really hungry.

   Definitive blue grouse cuisine, however, requires an open fire and a
nip in the air. Classically, blues should be served to bone-weary bow
hunters who would be ready to eat their boots if someone hadn't picked
up a couple of grouse on the way into camp. As the birds are prepared,
the conversation should focus on elk, and phrases such as "Just one more
step..." and "Then the damn wind..." should punctuate it regularly. The
subject of this ritual banter will be conspicuous by its absence from the
meat pole, which is why the main course features grouse in the first place.
Seared in an open skillet, the birds themselves should have the texture of
blackened redfish on the outside and sashimi on the inside, for that is
what happens to large fowl when they encounter hot cast iron.
Illuminated by dancing firelight, the hungry crew will pick the birds apart
with their fingers and wash them down with creek water or perhaps something a bit livelier, and when they finally crawl into their sleeping bags
and brace themselves against the chill, they will know that they have
eaten wild game as it was meant to be eaten.
   The blue grouse is consistent enough on the table. It saves its surprises for the field. On any given day, it is hard to know which version of the
blue might be waiting for you up there on the ridge tops. The bird suffers
from guilt by association. Mentally consign the blue to the fool hen category and you will have created a self-fulfilling prophecy, for that is the
only way you will ever see it. You will subliminally dismiss the sound of
those wild flushes and the flickering image of the bird hurtling through
the trees while you note and acknowledge the sight of the fool hen strutting along the ground or staring back at you from a branch a literal
stone's throw away. But if you load your gun and call your dog and set
off to hunt your way uphill through blue grouse country, you may never
forget the birds that you find.

Ten Pointers

There are few concepts in outdoor sport as predictably tiresome as the notion of the "Good Old Days," especially when evoked with a whine. Of course it would be wonderful to enjoy our favorite places the way they were before others came along and made them crowded, but longing for such circumstances is mostly a matter of selfishness. It is also a matter of naiveté, for the status of most North American wildlife has improved so consistently throughout this century that looking back is as likely to disappoint as to inspire, at least if done honestly. After a decade of drought, however, our waterfowl are hurting, and even though I still regard myself as a young man, I often find myself beginning conversations about duck hunting with worrisome expressions such as: "Why, I remember when..."

Few measures of my own wistful thinking about ducks are as precise and objective as the Central Flyway hundred-point limit. It is startling to realize how few years ago one could legally, ethically, and with full biological justification leave a prairie pothole with ten ducks hanging from the game strap at the end of the morning.

The point system has always had its detractors, of course, including hunters and non-hunters alike. Certainly some of us have difficulty making fast, accurate identifications on the wing, and there are those who contend, with at least some justification, that too many hunters can't tell the difference between a canvasback and a merganser in the hand, much less on the wing half an hour before sunrise. But for those who approach waterfowling with conviction, the point system has always been just one more skill to manage, one more perspective on the birds. To put it simply, mastering it is fun. And field identification can become another element in the friendly rivalries that always seem to thrive in duck blinds. If you announce at the start of the morning that you plan to shoot a pure limit of ten-point pintails and promptly dump a seventy-point blue crested mudsucker, you can damn well plan on hearing about it. You can also plan on eating roasted mudsucker that night as your companions enjoy more stately fare, at least if dinner is being served at our house.

A mixture of valid principle and popular misconception, the traditional Central Flyway hundred-point limit recognized four basic kinds of ducks: Prized Divers, Rare Oddballs, Mallards, and the Little Brown Ducks that included almost all the leftovers.

Canvasbacks and redheads—the Prized Divers—were assigned high point values on the basis of both historical stature and marginal populations, and it is hard to argue with either concept. While they didn't command the can's one hundred-point premium, Rare Oddballs could end a hunt with a careless shot or two, quite properly reflecting the idea that no one really needs to shoot a lot of hooded mergansers or ring-necked ducks.

It was the discrepancy between the point value of mallards and the Little Brown Ducks that always struck me as illogical. Drake mallards traditionally came with a twenty-point price tag while a hen would cost you seventy. There were certainly plenty of mallards, and in those bountiful days a five drake limit was actually quite conservative, especially in comparison to a legal bag of ten pintails.

The mallard's worth has always been inflated by its popular image as the quintessential American duck. Ask a sample of kids to draw a wild duck and there will be only two kinds of responses—mallards and mysteries. Examine the duck hunting features in most general-interest sporting magazines and what will you see in the pictures? Mallards, that's what; a steady, monotonous torrent of greenheads. Or how about this conversation, that I go through in some form or another almost every time I stop at a local cafe wearing camouflage after a morning on some pothole:

Casual Coffee Drinker: "Hey, Doc! Any northern mallards down yet?"

Your Correspondent: "Not a one. Nothing but those damn brown ducks."

Casual Coffee Drinker: "Then I may as well go watch the football game. Let me know when the northerns get here."

Your Correspondent: "You have my solemn word as a gentleman."

It is not my intention to disdain the mallard, but to celebrate all those other splendid puddle ducks that were historically lumped together, given a dime price tag, and dismissed as lesser game. The assumption underlying this value system was that it was somehow more desirable to take home five greenheads than a mixed bag of, say, wigeon and teal. Here at the hardcore heart of waterfowling, however, most of us would dispute that arbitrary appraisal. In fact, the element of variety that all those Little Brown Ducks provide is one reason prairie potholes are so much fun to hunt.

In the recent era of generous bag limits, ten-pointers held a practical appeal as well. While it was never essential to shoot a lot of birds, it was satisfying to bring home an honest ten-duck limit back when there were ducks enough to go around. If your identification skills faltered and your wingshooting didn't, there was nothing to do when the dog delivered that fat seventy-point hen mallard but call it a day and hope she tasted as good as seven blue-wings on the table. For those of us who enjoy setting our own standards, bucking the conventional obsession with mallards became its own reward. Above all, learning the ten-pointers allowed the opportunity to savor the unique character of each one of them, and in doing so I discovered qualities as distinctive as those of different vintage wines.

Here follow thumbnail sketches of some favorites:

Pintail

"Why are you so fascinated by pintails?" a visiting friend asked me one morning as we shared a blind in a local marsh. "To me they're just little brown ducks." (I am not making this up.)

To my surprise, I found that I had a difficult time explaining my feelings. I spoke of the pintail's linear grace without making any impression.

I went on about the drake's elegant tuxedo breeding plumage, another of those nowhere-else-in-nature marvels, and my friend shrugged his shoulders. Recognizing an impasse, for the rest of the morning I let him have the mallards while I concentrated on the pintails, and in the end we both went home happy.

I have since come to realize how much flying airplanes helps to define an appreciation for the pintail. No other duck demonstrates such a marvelous command of the air. Consider a flock of gold-standard mallards flying high over a spread of decoys with the wind behind them. If one decides to come in to the blocks, it will typically make a gentle turn, establish a controlled descent, and finally touch down with all the imagination and style of a 747 landing at LAX.

Now contrast this style of flight to the pintail's. At the moment of decision, a pintail will characteristically drop its upwind wing near vertical, apply opposite rudder, and begin a full flaps, side-slipping freefall guaranteed to make your mouth drop. During the vertiginous descent, the roar of air through all those primaries can make a peaceful duck marsh sound like a jet propulsion laboratory. At the last minute, the bird will do something magical with those airfoils, and if you are too enthralled to stand and shoot, as I sometimes am, you can just sit and watch as it settles onto the water with all the grace of a falling cherry blossom. How can anyone fail to be fascinated by a bird such as this?

As limits go, the ten-point pintail was the biggest bargain on the prairie. If pintails had been stocks, analysts would have called them seriously undervalued. It all comes back to that Little Brown Duck nonsense. If pintails had pink heads, they would probably make the magazine covers, too.

Unfortunately, the resourceful pintail breeds in marginal water of the kind that has been hit hardest by the drought. Pintail numbers are down precipitously at the time of this writing. I stopped feeling good about shooting them several years ago, so now I just look. That is an honest enough sentiment, born of the notion that if you are going to shoot a lot during times of plenty, you should exercise restraint during times of need. Such restraint may be even stricter than the limits of the law itself, and that's the way it is with pintails now, at least for me.

They will return. I believe that. In the meantime, the sight of a drake's elegantly stenciled neck in spring or the sound of a flock's

descent into a prairie pothole at sundown will just have to do, and somehow it always does.

Gadwall

Perhaps it is the gadwall that comes closest to defining the unheralded
ten-pointer. Its traditional gunner's name—gray mallard—manages to do
an injustice to two species at once. In fact, the drake gadwall, a handsome though subtle specimen, is scarcely gray at all. The chestnut wing
markings are marvelous and you can lose yourself in that beautiful, mottled pattern on the belly if you stare at it for a minute or two.

Gadwall are an early season staple here on the prairie. Light and
graceful in the air, they respond readily to decoys, which they often
approach in large, homogeneous flocks. On more than one early October
morning, I have set out with the express purpose of taking a pure ten-bird
limit of gadwalls and done just that.

There is little that is spectacular about the gadwall, but there is little
that is disappointing either. On a personal level, gadwalls define the
small prairie pothole habitat of northeastern Montana and there are few
places of which I would rather be reminded. Gadwalls saved the day for
me there so many times that it would seem rude not to give them the
respect they have earned.

Wigeon

Let us be precise and specify that we are talking about the American
wigeon. There is an Old World variety that occasionally shows up as a
stray on both coasts, but I have never seen one. The familiar baldpate is
another story.

One afternoon far from home, while I was on my way to a medical
meeting, I noticed flocks of ducks insistently working what turned out to
be nothing more than a two-acre patch of wet grass. Since the meeting
wasn't that important (are they ever?) and since I always have the essen-
tials with me during hunting season, I was soon hunkered down at the
edge of the grass with my gun in my hand and a half-dozen decoys in
front of me, listing foolishly on their useless keels. I even had Sky with
me that day, which illustrates the important principle that one should
never go anywhere without a Labrador retriever, especially during hunting
season. The amateur quality of our decoy spread didn't seem to matter.
The ducks—wigeons, flocks and flocks of wigeons—all wanted to land

precisely on that patch of abandoned pasture and nowhere else. I collected a wigeon dinner from the first set. Since that was all I could handle under the circumstances, I just sat in the weeds and watched as the rest of them poured in. The air was full of noise, from the ducks' wings and their three-note whistles, and it saddened me to realize that somewhere down the road several dozen reasonable people were sitting in a windowless room working intently, with no dogs to keep them company and without a single wigeon overhead.

I never did make it to that meeting.

Blue-Winged Teal

Now on to matters even closer to the heart, if that is possible.

One of the great humiliations I ever endured with a shotgun in my hands came courtesy of the diminutive blue-wing. We had constructed a series of blinds that summer on a shallow lake in a remote corner of the prairie. The entire lake is gone now, for the same climactic reasons there are no true ten-pointers anymore, but at the time it was the focus of a broad, fertile wetland that provided breeding habitat for thousands of virtually unhunted ducks.

The reeds grew high that season and wading through the muck in the early morning darkness was like entering a jungle warfare theater. As shooting light finally spilled over the horizon, the teal arrived in tight, uniform flocks of eight to twelve birds each. Flying fast and low, they would appear suddenly over the tops of the reeds and gun their way across the opening in front of the blind just daring you to fire both barrels before they disappeared. And fire I did. As we left the truck that morning, I had stuffed a handful of shells in my vest with a haughty aside to my partners asking how many shells they thought I needed to shoot a limit of teal. By the time the sun cleared the horizon, there were nearly two dozen empties floating around inside the blind while a grand total of one blue-wing rested beside me on the seat. The dog's attitude had changed from sympathy to disgust. My hunting partners were in another blind a half-mile away, so there were no other witnesses. Hoping that difficulties of their own had kept them from counting shots, I snuck back to the truck for more shells. By the end of the morning, I had a teal dinner without much to spare. That evening, the duck sauce was thickened with humility and heavily flavored with respect.

Beautiful on the water, graceful in the air, a challenge to any gunner and a delicate mouthful for an eager dog or a hungry hunter, the blue-winged teal would seem to have it all. Indeed it does, all except for size, which for some reason matters terribly to certain people. I appreciate size when the quarry is a whitetail or a ram, but a duck?

"Why do you even bother with those things?" I recall one curmudgeonly old hunting partner asking me one day. "You can eat one in two bites!"

That's not much of an exaggeration, but what bites they will be. For those who truly love their duck on the table, the blue-wing offers succulence that cannot be duplicated. The mere thought of a rack of blue-wings disappearing into a hot oven is enough to make me cancel engagements and lie to my friends.

Two bites, ten points...it's still one hell of a deal.

Shoveler

Some things are funny even though they don't mean to be: moose calves, Edsels, the United States Congress, North Dakota. To this distinguished list I would add the last of our ten-pointers, the shoveler.

It's not that the poor shoveler plays the kazoo or walks like Charlie Chaplin in The Little Tramp. In fact, on the wing the shoveler is a delicate bird that flies like a cross between a teal and a pintail. Furthermore, the drake shoveler in his spring breeding plumage is one of the most handsome birds on the prairie. But there is the unavoidable matter of the shoveler's bill.

It's hard to say just why the shoveler's snout is so comical. Certainly those who equate function with beauty shouldn't be laughing. When it comes to dredging up goobers from the bottom of a pond, this design would be hard to improve upon. But there it is coming at you like Cyrano's nose, and every time the dog hands you a spoonbill, you must somehow come to terms with its appearance.

Lone shovelers have a habit of tagging along with flocks of other waterfowl. I have a friend (who shall remain nameless) with an uncanny ability to isolate and drop, by accident, the one shoveler from a flock of almost anything else. I swear that he once used his second barrel to pluck a shoveler from a flock of honkers as they flared over our blind, although he still insists that my dog somehow conjured the fallen duck from the marsh by magic. I have watched him make remarkable shots on spoonbills even as he missed mallards, pintails, and geese at closer ranges—and when one of the dogs returns to the blind with a shoveler in its mouth, even the Chessies know where to deliver it.

Over the years it has been my pleasure to salute these accomplishments by preparing his shovelers in many imaginative disguises: shoveler *l'orange*, shoveler stuffed with wild rice and apricots, honey smoked shoveler...the list goes on. One thing all this has taught me is that there is nothing wrong with shovelers on the table, their lightweight reputation there notwithstanding. Despite its omnivorous diet (never examine the stomach contents of a shoveler unless you plan to serve it to someone you dislike), properly prepared shoveler is nothing to get snooty about.

Yet for no real reason I avoid shooting them. Somehow I always wind up thinking of shovelers as comic relief and it's hard to haul off and throw a load of shot at something that reminds you of Groucho Marx. Perhaps it is my imagination, but I swear that when one of the experienced Labs brings a shoveler to the blind, he looks embarrassed.

I prefer to imagine the shoveler in the springtime, as a non-combatant, with no guns or dogs involved. Then if you get close enough and hold still enough, the drake's yellow eye will shine at you like a jewel and remind you in one glance why wetlands are worth worrying about.

Rather selfishly, I am glad the current duck crisis has come at a time when I have already taken my share of them. The rules of engagement are different now, and today thoughtful waterfowlers operate under the principles of voluntary restraint. I only set out the decoys once this year. On opening day, I shot a limit of blue-wings. Now that the drought has increased their point value from ten to thirty-five, that limit consisted of three birds.

Since I knew in my heart that I was done for the season, I treated my three teal with ritual respect. I roasted them simply, with nothing but a dash of salt between the birds and my palate. I did not offer to share them with anyone. In fact, our company dined on sharptail that evening as I polished off all three teal without apology.

It may seem facile to reduce a sense of loss to simple numbers. The numbers are there, however, and they linger fresh enough in the memory to remind us all how recently the West was full of water and the ducks that thrive upon it. There is no reason why we should not reflect upon such matters as we wait for the prairie to bloom again.

White Birds, Just Right

North of the 60th parallel, there are few sounds as reassuring as the steady throb of a Lycoming engine. Each one feels just a little different than all the rest and after a while you learn the nuances of your own and those of your friends. On this particularly brilliant winter day, I was delighted to hear mine sounding just the way it should. It was bitterly cold despite the sun and below me the vast foothills of the Alaska Range stretched away in all directions, all but monotonous in their splendor. I could hear Sky panting contentedly from his familiar perch on the Cub's back seat, and I almost imagined that he was searching, too.

We were hunting ptarmigan. Cynics might insist that we were road hunting and I suppose that we were in a way. At least we were doing so in a uniquely Alaskan fashion. At that time of year ptarmigan are concentrated in widely scattered flocks, and since it can be a long way between birds and Alaska's same-day-airborne law doesn't apply to small game, I have never been opposed to scouting them from the air.

White birds on snow, of course, are hard enough to see from the ground, let alone from one hundred feet above it while passing by at ninety miles per hour. It is possible to cruise along just above the willows and spot them out the window, but the natural history of pilots who fly low and slow while concentrating on anything other than flying is eventual disaster. The end result is all too often what is known locally as the moose hunter's stall—not the kind of aviation mishap that people often walk away from.

Because my hunting partners and I all look forward to many seasons yet to come, we have developed our own technique for finding ptarmigin from the air. This method employs one pilot as a bird dog. Cruising just over the brush, his job is to flush rather than to look. The second aircraft trails behind at a safer altitude and watches for birds as they rise behind the leader. And that explains why my friend Joe Sangster was flying along the willows like some winged parody of a springer spaniel while I followed behind with the relative luxury of two hundred feet of air between me and the cold, hard ground.

We had covered miles of country without seeing a bird, which wasn't to say that there was a shortage of interesting things outside the window. Great glaciers descended the flanks of volcanic peaks to the west and the sun and the clear sky offered a belated promise that the long northern winter would someday end. There were moose yarded up in the willows and their dark forms stood out so implausibly against the snow that it was hard to remember how difficult it could be to find one in September. There were wolf tracks down there, too, and while I sometimes find myself with strange bedfellows in opposition to Alaska's aerial wolf hunting laws, I always watched for wolves when I flew, just because I enjoyed seeing them.

Then I noticed a brief flutter in the snow behind Joe's airplane, as if a small gathering of people had waved white handkerchiefs at a boat departing from a dock. "White birds," I told Joe over the radio as I banked hard and tried to commit the rapidly disappearing landscape to memory.

"Okee-doke," Joe replied in his transplanted Georgia drawl. Of course that is what Joe would say in response to anything over the radio, whether it was the announcement that I had spotted a bull moose or experienced an engine failure.

We circled and set up to land on a frozen slough. There is always a moment of anxiety when you transfer the airplane's weight from wings to skis, but the Cub coasted gently to a stop and there it was—the great, overwhelming silence that reaches out and grabs you whenever an airplane's engine shuts down in the bush.

The dogs jumped forth eagerly and peed their way around the airplanes, weaving great yellow circles through the snow. After tying the engine covers over the cowlings, we set off across the slough. Twenty yards later I was regretting the decision not to bring snowshoes. "Now where did you mark those birds?" Joe asked.

I studied the mute lines of willow ahead of us. It had been so obvious from the air, but the descent to ground-level had cost me that perspective and now the tundra wrapped around us in a vast blanket of featureless terrain. "Right over there," I replied with what I hoped sounded like confidence. "Between the slough and the river."

The snow was perfectly wrong. It had set up hard, but the crust wasn't strong enough to hold our weight and walking through it felt like working out on some merciless exercise machine. Occasionally we found a lead of wind-packed snow that we could walk on and the progress was exhilarating until we started to break through again. The dogs were faring better than we were, since there was enough crust to support them. Glad to be free of the airplanes, they scampered about happily and looked back from time to time as if they could not imagine what was taking us so long to catch up.

As we approached the patch of willows where I thought I had marked the birds, a reedy chuckle sounded from the brush and then a vast swell of wingbeats flooded the winter air. Clouds of ptarmigin rose in front of us like an avalanche falling in reverse. The birds were all flushing wild, but we held our fire, certain that there would be stragglers.

We bracketed the cover and began to work it toward the river. Ptarmigan continued to spew forth in unbelievable numbers, but they were hopelessly spooky. I watched them sail off across the landscape by the hundreds until one finally flushed at the edge of shooting range. The bird was plainly visible against a dark background of brush when it rocketed up from its hiding place, but just as I caught up with the gun barrel, it cut across a brilliantly lit snowfield and simply vanished. I shot where I thought the bird was going to be but nothing happened, and the escaping ptarmigan's hoarse cry sounded like mockery in the frigid air.

This madness went on for another half-mile. Every bird in the valley seemed to have chosen this particular willow patch for a winter home, but they were utterly crazy. I snapped off another shot or two at marginal ranges, but I just couldn't track the birds against the snow and I didn't cut a feather. Finally, after we turned back toward the slough, we did what we should have done in the first place, which was to isolate a strip of brush and work toward each other from opposite directions. Halfway through the cover, Joe pushed a single over my head. The bird stood out like a pearl against the cerulean sky and I dropped it easily. The dog seemed painfully relieved by this accomplishment and presented the bird like an undeserved consolation prize. When we finally arrived back at the ski tracks on the slough, that single ptarmigan was all we had to show for our efforts.

"Tell me, Joe," I said, because I needed some independent verification of events, "Do you think we flushed a thousand birds out there?"

"I believe we did," he replied.

"You ever see anything quite like that before?"

"Never."

Joe was a veteran of many seasons in Alaska and it relieved me to know that he regarded this experience as exceptional, because I did not think I could stand this on a regular basis.

As we fumbled with the engine covers and prepared to depart, I wondered, as I had so many times before, what I had to do in order to come to terms with ptarmigan on the wing.

There are three species of ptarmigan to be found in North America. Although I am an enthusiastic amateur naturalist and more interested in these things than most people, I will admit that I have trouble telling them apart. I can do it when I try, but there is a generic similarity among the species—mottled in the summer and almost unnaturally white in the winter—that makes it easy to lump them all together as just plain ptarmigan. Alaska's schoolchildren wisely chose the willow ptarmigan as the official state bird, and they were the ones that drove Joe Sangster and me nuts that afternoon on the west side of Cook Inlet. The rock and white-tailed varieties are equally capable of provocation.

My first encounters with Alaska ptarmigan took place in late summer, before there was snow on the ground, and they were different birds then. Like sharptails, which they resemble in many ways, ptarmigan remain organized in family groups until fall. During August, when I often ran into them while bowhunting for caribou and sheep, they were well camouflaged but often naive to the point of brainlessness. Summer birds are virtually impossible to see when hunkered down on the tundra, but they seem to lack confidence in their ability to remain hidden. As you approach, they usually start to fidget and cluck, and they soon wind up looking very much like archery targets. Since these breakdowns in discipline often take place within bow range, and since ptarmigan taste far better than the usual freeze-dried sheep-camp fare, such behavior was perfectly welcome at the time, even if it was hard to get excited about mounting a major expedition for summer ptarmigan with dog and gun.

Tundra chickens in August, white maniacs in February—there had to be some sort of middle ground and I was determined to find it. I didn't miss much about the Lower 48 when I lived in Alaska, but I did miss bird hunting, which is akin to saying that I miss my wife and children or my right arm. My dogs were turning into potlickers, grown bored and lazy through seasons of disuse after their full-throttle upbringing on the plains of Montana. The thought that Sky might die without making one more real bird hunt was in itself grounds for depression. And there was nothing wrong with ptarmigan. They really did remind me of the sharptails I missed so badly, and they inhabited wild and wonderful places that could be enjoyed with the flimsiest excuse. All I had to do was find them when they were being gamebirds and behaving just right.

I took up the search in earnest the following autumn. As usual, I had thumped a ptarmigan dinner or two while bowhunting, but that didn't count. I wanted to react to the sound of wings and perform the mental exercise of picking one bird from a flock, to heft my double, and watch the dog surge ahead with the sort of enthusiasm that no mere training dummy could ever provide. And I thought I knew just where I might make all these things happen.

I had encountered ptarmigan in this particular mountain pass three years earlier. That had been my first season in Alaska, which explains why I was foolish enough to be miles back in the high country on my horse during the last week in October. The trip had been equal measures of stupidity and blind enthusiasm. The day I ran into the ptarmigan I was packing out a large bull caribou I had shot the previous evening. The snow was up to the horses' bellies by the time we reached the pass, and things were going so badly that when the birds started to erupt from the brush along the trail, I scarcely paid any attention to them. But I marked the pass and the birds it contained the same way I mark other fragments of data that might someday be turned into hunts.

There was no place to land an airplane on the mountain, so we had to drive to the base and hike a steep seven miles to the pass. Snow had fallen and melted and frozen again and the footing was terrible. But the chances of the mountain killing us if we hiked up it were less than the chances of cabin fever killing us if we didn't, so Alex Russell, Joe Kelly, and I loaded our packs with shotgun shells and lunch and started eagerly up the trail.

Of all the remarkable things about Alaska, none is more remarkable than the quality of its light, which is unlike that found anywhere else. We started the climb in a layer of ice fog. The low sun on the southern horizon made the fog glow luminously and the light had an odd, non-directional quality to it that made it impossible for our eyes to determine which way was up. But our legs knew, and we climbed on across the icy rocks with the weather's eerie glow locked all around us.

In Europe, I am told, slings are standard equipment on shotguns as well as rifles, and two miles into the hike I began to appreciate why. In places, I needed two hands to climb and two more to hold my shotgun, and something had to give. Finally it did, and when my beloved double fell onto a shard of rock, the forestock splintered with a sickening crunch. We all gathered round and studied the damage with sadness, but there was nothing to do except to keep hiking. At least I had the foresight to gather the stock's splintered remains and store them in the lunch bag inside my pack. For the rest of the day, the gun felt unnatural when I held it in my left hand and my fingers closed on cold metal where worn, familiar wood should have been.

We grew too tired to talk and continued in silence. The dog stopped exploring the trail ahead and fell into place beside me. The ice underfoot became snow, which rose farther and farther up our legs as we drew closer to the pass. There are people who would be busy asking if I were sure this was the place I had seen the ptarmigan, meaning that they reserved the right to be pissy if we didn't find any, but Joe and Alex are not that kind of people, which is why they were there with me in the first place. Five miles up the trail, it occurred to me that the search for true wingshooting in Alaska was beginning to take on the character of an epic.

Then the sun began to brighten and suddenly we climbed out of the fog layer. The mountains around us became sharp and clear as jewels. I could see the pass ahead of us at last, and the same scrub brush that had held the ptarmigan three seasons earlier. We stopped and had a bite to eat and talked to the dogs the way a coach might talk to his players before an important game, and then we unpacked our game vests and loaded our guns and continued on toward the brush and the Great Perhaps.

Ahead of me, Sky suddenly became interested in the rare mountain air. Then the welcome sound of wings rose from the cover, accompanied by the reedy call of ptarmigan. A bird flushed right in front of me, splendidly white against the polarized blue of the arctic sky. For a moment I was so overjoyed that I almost forgot to shoot. Then my instincts asserted themselves. I swung and the bird crumpled and the dog danced happily across the snow toward the fall. When he returned with the bird, he seemed to be holding his head higher than he had in years.

More birds rose farther up the sidehill and I heard the others fire, exchange excited shouts, and fire again. The dog and I moved forward through the snow drifts and another covey flushed from the next clump of bushes. Remembering my misadventures of the previous winter, I concentrated on nothing but their dark outer tailfeathers as the birds roared across the snow. That kept me from lifting my head in a futile search for the whole bird and when I shot, the tailfeathers simply disappeared from the air. The dog broke eagerly from my side as I concentrated on the second half of the double and it did not even occur to me to correct him.

And so it went for an hour, as fast an hour as I have ever spent in the field. There was a twenty-ptarmigan limit in effect, and yes, I filled it. Greedy? I don't think so. We had worked hard for those birds, and I was learning important things about myself on the mountain that day. Infatuated as most new arrivals are by Alaska's big game, I had been away from the shotgun for too long, and if it took a limit of ptarmigan to prove the point, so be it. And if I shot for no other reason than to see the look on the dog's face, it all would have been worthwhile.

My limit of birds weighed considerably more than the box of shells it took to shoot them, and my knees measured every ounce of our success on the trip down the mountain. The arctic daylight cut us short as it usually does in the winter, and we stumbled down the last mile of the trail in darkness. At the trailhead, I had to lift the dog into the truck and I would not have objected if someone had done the same for me.

On the way home, we stopped in Cooper Landing where I looked up my old friend and master gunsmith, Bill Fuller. I handed Bill the shotgun and the bag of wood fragments and asked him to do what he could with it. Today I still delight in studying that rebuilt forestock and trying to find the seams that Bill's skilled hands made all but invisible. I can see them if I look hard enough, and every time I do I am reminded of why I loved Alaska and why I left it, and of the day when I finally found the ptarmigan just right.

Soul Chickens

No experience defines the concept of wide-open spaces quite like a long, solitary walk across the eastern Montana prairie in September, especially if you are looking for something that you cannot find. Here the landscape seems to wither beneath the sun, and it is difficult to remember that a few weeks ago everything was green and in a few weeks more everything will be white, because today it is all so relentlessly brown. Overhead, the cloudless sky just couldn't get any bigger and the earth seems to stretch its shoulders an extra measure of distance toward the horizon in order to accommodate it. There are more ups and downs here than flat land is supposed to be able to manage. I'm glad of that. The terrain keeps its own secrets—in this case between the birds and those who care enough to hunt them.

Today I am the one doing the looking, and the something I cannot find is a sharptail grouse. The dog and I have covered a good two miles since we left the truck. They were easy miles by the standards of last week's elk hunt, but it is getting hot and the dog is panting and it is only a matter of time until I will be panting, too. There have been jackrabbits, antelope, and a rattlesnake this morning and I am glad to have seen them all, even the snake, which was too small and docile to have caused any real alarm. Nonetheless, it's about time for some birds.

Perhaps it is the sense of emptiness out here that always makes a sharptail covey's rise so dramatic—that and the noise they make when you find and flush them at last. Cock pheasants sound angry when they take to the air and Huns sound fast, but flushing sharptails sound like God just rolled the dice. This morning's first close encounter proves true to form. One minute I am alone with the dog and the silence and then a roll of thunder rises from the grass, all wingbeat and the rich, throaty chuckle that fixes the sharptail's identity at once for the experienced prairie gunner. By the time the first two birds clear the ground cover and reach up into the sky, they belong to me, and then to the Parker, and then to the dog, and finally to me again, at least for a little while.

And what a pair of birds they are up close: solid and chunky, organized more compactly about their own center of gravity than most gamebirds and dressed in plumage so intricately patterned you can forget for a
moment that it doesn't contain a lick of color other than gray and black
and tan. Birds like this appeal to the soul. They even smell good, to me
as well as to the dog, and I can already imagine this pair on the table and
how they will remind me all over again that sharptails taste as good as
they look and sound on the wing.

There will be more shooting on the long walk back to the truck.
There will be hits and misses and dog work, the conventional parameters
of the gunner's sport. But it is the birds that I have come for today, the
sharptails and the country that they live in, and not even the snappiest
double or most heroic retrieve can finally distract from that purpose.

God, I just love it out here.

It is time for a confession: as far as I'm concerned, sharptails are about
the most wonderful thing that ever grew feathers, laid an egg, or flew
without a propeller. Anyone interested in a calculated, objective evalua-
tion of the species as a gamebird is going to have to look for it somewhere else. I spent a long time trying to think of something unkind to say
about the sharptail just to give this discussion some pretense of balance,
but I couldn't come up with anything. Honest.

First, a definition of terms. There are no prairie chickens in Montana,
but you can't tell that to any of the local ranchers in my part of the world,
to whom all gamebirds except waterfowl and cock pheasants are "chickens." At least in the sharptail's case the term is descriptive. They do look
like chickens, drably colored and round in the middle with stubby points
at each end. Good thing, since I surrendered to local vernacular decades
ago and have been joyously yelling "Chickens!" at flushing sharptails
ever since. This habit can be a source of distress to visiting friends unfamiliar with western wingshooting, who often stand there wondering if I
am pointing out greater prairie chickens or lesser prairie chickens or misplaced barnyard chickens until the birds are out of range or I have abandoned all pretense of etiquette and shot them out from under my guests.
Eventually, such visitors either catch on and start yelling "Chickens!" and
shooting some birds themselves, or they go home empty-handed and perplexed by the whole experience.

While the sharptail is the definitive prairie gamebird to those of us who know it, most American gunners don't. The problem is largely geographic. The sharptail's natural habitat is the sub-arctic steppe, and south of the Canadian border its range is limited to out-of-the-way corners of our own Great Plains. On the positive side, sharptails do just fine in terrain that does not lend itself to cultivation, which means that there are plenty of them to be found and hunted on public rangeland, an important consideration for visitors without benefit of access to private property. And unlike such flashy imports as the ringneck and the Hun, the sharptail's claim to the prairie carries the weight of historical authority.

I live in sharptail country, and the fact that there are sharptails in the place I've chosen to call home is no accident. I've tried living without sharptails, but I just didn't like it. How can a simple gamebird exert so much influence over an ordinarily level-headed guy like me? As Elizabeth Barret Browning said, let me count the ways...

I love the way chickens cooperate for dogs. They rarely run and seem to hold forever, at least in the early season when the cover is thick and the birds are organized in familial coveys. They are tractable enough to allow a young dog frequent rewards for its efforts. They don't humiliate dogs the way ringnecks often do and they don't bore them like sage hens. My dogs always seem pleased with themselves when they have sharptails in their mouths. Evidently this form of canine happiness is contagious to humans.

I love sharptails on the table. I enjoy them there because they are unique, just the way doves and woodcock and teal are unique when served to an appreciative audience of hungry hunters. We eat an awful lot of pheasant at our house, and as much as I enjoy pheasant on the table, it begins to lose its sense of character after a while. Spend some time with the sauces and you can serve pheasant to anyone, even unsuspecting guests who might dither unbearably if they knew they were eating something that didn't come from the supermarket. Sharptail, in contrast, is always distinctive—some would say distinctive to a fault, but that is their problem. The fact remains that when young sharptails are cooked properly, wild game on the table doesn't get any better.

I love the way sharptails develop their character during the course of the season, a process that expands the challenge they provide as gamebirds. In September, you may have to walk a long way to find them, but when you do, they can be relied upon to cooperate. Give them a couple of months and they can become different birds entirely.

Last November, I took an afternoon off from the pursuit of deer with my bow for the express purpose of shooting a limit of late season sharptails. The weather was flirting with the transition from fall to winter. A skiff of snow clung to the edges of the prairie and the unstable sky overhead sent gusts of wind howling down the coulees to challenge my woolens. With the advent of the whitetail rut, my Labs had been reduced to the status of house dogs, but Sonny seemed to note with interest the inclusion of the shotgun when I loaded the truck, and now he was bouncing along eagerly at my side, as happy as a kid out of school.

We set off across the open toward a distant line of brush, where I hoped to find some birds willing to hold for us. Suddenly a large group of sharptails flushed wild from the grass over a hundred yards away. There were at least sixty birds in the flock. After the initial chaotic rise, they made a downwind turn and then sailed along in unison with their characteristic flutter-and-glide wingbeat pattern until they disappeared into the featureless background of the prairie.

I carefully marked the spot where they had risen from the sweep of snow and dried grass ahead, and with the dog hacked in tightly to heel, we set out to look for stragglers. There was one, as there almost always is. The dog nosed the bird into the air near the margin of my range and it dropped a leg at the sound of the Parker's report. The bird set its wings and rode the air and came down finally in a distant tangle of wild roses. The dog stayed close to my side as we hiked across the open grass together. I kept the shotgun ready when I sent him into the thorny strip of cover in case the bird flushed again, but when he finally pounced, the grouse was dead as a stone. Although less than a perfectly satisfying kill, I enjoyed the feel of the bird in the game bag as we started walking once again.

Another flock of chickens rose wild ahead of us as we continued on toward the heavy cover, but this time they did not even bother to leave a straggler. I marked the flock down in the brush a mile or so away, and when we finally reached the cover, I turned in that direction, hoping that the birds might hold in the thick canopy of the bushes. When a single finally flushed, however, it was nearly out of range, and I just plain missed.

By the time we reached the area where the flock had set in, I could see a single sharptail perched warily in the top of a dead cottonwood tree and I knew that we were doomed. Such birds have but one function—to serve as sentries. This bird knew its job description well. We were still out of shotgun range when it chattered its way into the sky, and the rest of the flock rose from the ground beneath the cottonwood and followed the leader toward the distant horizon. They didn't leave any stragglers this time either.

Again I marked the flock down in the distance. I looked at my watch and thought about the whitetail stand I planned to occupy at sundown and the long walk back to the truck. We were having friends over that evening. I had promised everyone a sharptail dinner and the solitary bird resting in the game bag was beginning to feel less like a triumph than an embarrassment. My culinary imagination wrestled desperately with the impossible algebra of one sharptail and four hungry adults. Grouse soup? Wild rice casserole with sharptail and something from a can? Prairie chicken pie? I might never hear the end of this. Heeding the tug of my own pride, I set off across the prairie with renewed determination and the ever-willing dog at my side.

On their second wild flush, the flock had set in along a line of thorn apple bushes. Once again, birds rose out of range as Sonny and I approached. Some of their original number seemed to be missing this time, however, and I urged the Lab into the brush with more optimism than I had felt all afternoon.

This time the roar of beating wings felt close and explosive, like a promise fulfilled. The first bird borrowed a trick from the eastern ruffed grouse playbook and kept a dense screen of brush between us until it was out of range. The next pair was not so lucky. When the dog flushed them, they erupted from my side of the brush patch and provided an easy double.

I still needed one more bird to complete my limit and satisfy the evening's social demands. When Sonny had finished the second retrieve, I sent him back into the cover, but this time the bushes remained silent. My pride was still too aroused to concede the need for an awkward division of three grouse among four people at the dinner table that night, so I shouldered the double and set off after the wild bunch one more time.

I had only marked their general route of flight, and after a half-hour of hunting it was apparent that they had eluded us. The sky was turning pink in the west by the time I gave up and turned back toward the truck. There would be no deer hunt that evening. The temperature was dropping by now and the wind felt as if it meant business. The dog jumped a covey of Huns on the walk back and I made the front half of the potential double, as the rest of the birds rode the breeze beyond shotgun range. I told myself that it was too late to chase the Huns, but the truth of the matter was that I was too cold, too tired, and probably just too old. Back at the truck, I kenneled Sonny and spread our mixed bag out to air, thankful that one of our visitors that evening preferred Huns to grouse. Despite my obligations as host, I wasn't surrendering my chicken dinner to anyone.

I love sharptails in the spring. Except for turkeys, we don't think much about gamebirds at that time of year, which is largely a function of narrow-mindedness on our own part. It's certainly a mistake to think that the birds we love to hunt in the fall aren't doing anything interesting until then.

Now it is early May. I have been getting up in the dark for so many mornings in a row that the alarm's mindless bleat seems as natural as the sunrise due to follow. That is the kind of obsessive dedication that comes when you do your turkey hunting with a longbow, but the turkeys are another story, and this morning I have simpler pleasures in mind.

Rain fell yesterday, but the thirsty prairie consumed this offering at once and there is nothing left behind but an elusive cleanliness in the air. I leave the truck at the second gate and walk the last hundred yards to the blind in the dark. Then there is nothing left to do but set up the camera and the tripod and settle into the business of waiting.

Waiting is an art in its own right, and doing the things I love to do outdoors has made me something of an expert. I spend a lot of time in the field waiting, and in contrast to waiting for antelope or whitetail bucks, this morning's exercise offers the luxury of being a relatively certain thing. And sure enough, I have scarcely settled into the simple hypnosis of being there when the prairie outside the blind comes alive with noise and there they are.

The sharptail lek is one of the great displays in nature. How the birds return so accurately to the same dancing grounds year after year remains a mystery, but they have done it again, right on schedule, three dozen eager males competing for position and the eventual favor of the hens. As if on cue, they inflate their brilliant purple neck sacs, tip forward like drunks, extend their wings, and dance. Several of them are hurtling about wildly now right in front of the blind, their feathered feet a blur of motion, the air alive with the wild staccato rhythm of their music. After several minutes of frenzy, the dancing stops and the birds settle into the grass to coo softly at each other and wait for the inspiration to begin dancing again.

The glowing sky reminds me that I've got things to do out here, but my light meter tells me what I already know, which is that I will have to keep on waiting. Somewhere near the edge of the action, one bird starts to stutter and the impulse spreads like a flame through spilled gasoline. Then the birds are all nuts again, seized by the psychotic impulse to do whatever it takes to contribute to the gene pool. Meanwhile, I must sit quietly inside the blind and wait for light that may not come in time.

Finally the sun spills over the horizon behind me, pushing the blind's shadow a hundred yards away across the prairie. I stare hungrily through the view finder, turn knobs, focus. Before I can do anything, however, it is too late. All the dancing has stopped and the birds are bleeding off into the grass in all directions. The spell has broken; the dance is over. The dancers are simply sharptails once again, and I am simply an observer, with a camera full of empty film. I will have to settle for the knowledge that this has all been recorded directly in the soul.

But what I love above all else about sharptail grouse is the country they inhabit. As a mental exercise, I sat down and tried to remember the last time I flushed a chicken in a place I didn't like. The list of possibilities included swales so thick with native grass that you could hardly drag your feet through the ground cover, buffalo berry bushes shimmering green and silver beneath an Indian summer sun, fields of golden stubble with wild roses clutching at their edges, and windblown prairie stretching away forever beneath the sky. Forget about people. Here the cast of characters consists of antelope rutting on distant ridges, bedded mulies exploding from the cover at your feet, coyotes howling at the rising sun, and raptors hunting overhead. Too few of us know these obscure corners of America, for the prairie's good or for our own.

I wouldn't have missed this country for the world, but without the sharptail I might never have managed to find it.

Small Water

There are several mechanisms by which standing water accumulates on the surface of the prairie, where water is often in scarce supply.

During wet years, low spots can sometimes gather enough run-off to become ponds in their own right. Give them a season or two and aquatic plants will appear around their margins as if by magic, even in the middle of barren plains or cultivated fields. It has never been clear to me just how this happens, but I suspect that ducks and other waterbirds must be involved in the transport of seeds to these remote wetlands. Of course, nesting waterfowl themselves ultimately benefit from these transplants, proving once again that nature is more than capable of looking out for its own, if people are willing to get out of the way long enough to let it happen.

Here in the coulee country of eastern Montana, where there is plenty of contour to the land, ponds often owe their existence to human intrusion. There is just something about steep-sided draws that makes cattlemen act like beavers in the exercise of some primal instinct to arrest the flow of water. Some of the older dams were failures, pushed up decades ago for reasons that no one can remember anymore. Now they stand as sage-studded monuments to homesteads gone bust beneath the relentless sun. Others provide important sources of water for livestock and wildlife to this day. Given the right wind, the dams can provide great cover for jump shooting ducks, should it come down to that. With their abrupt contours and sparse aquatic vegetation, however, the ponds themselves often suggest their artificial origins a bit too readily to provide classic waterfowl shooting. That is our problem, of course; such aesthetic liabilities are of little consequence to the ducks.

Finally there are the true potholes, formed by clear water percolating to the surface of the prairie like bubbles in a glass of champagne. Their precise origins are complex, but generally depend upon the exposure of porous, moisture-rich aquifers to the surface. The result of this sudden intrusion of water into the world of cactus and sage is almost always a wonderful surprise to anyone who appreciates the ability of wildlife to take advantage of small favors.

You can visit potholes during different seasons and enjoy something new every time. During the spring migration, a two-acre pothole can provide a morning's workout with binoculars and field guide as waterbirds of all kinds surge northward on the tide of lengthening days. Return a few weeks later and you will find all that frenzied excitement transformed into domesticity, with everything from dragonflies to shovelers caught up in the easy rhythms of procreation. Come back in the winter and the place will seem deserted. It might take some effort to imagine life incubating beneath the ice, but it is there. You can count on that.

However, there is no time to come to terms with a pothole quite like early autumn. This is a splendid season on the prairie, a time of pleasant days and crisp nights, with rich, warm colors everywhere for the eye to feast upon. A sense of purpose pervades the prairie, as those species that plan to leave prepare for their departure, while those that mean to stay ready themselves for the long, cold siege to come. Seldom is the essential relationship between beauty and its own demise more apparent.

For those of us who hunt, this is the special season, a time that demands more than simple contemplation. I suspect it has something to do with the pineal gland and the hypothalamus, the components of the vertebrate neuro-endocrine system that translate changes in the day-night cycle into various calls to action. The shortening of the days certainly seems to act as a command to everything else out there, from bugs to ducks to muskrats. Is it really any wonder that we too have instincts to obey?—to rise in the dark, gird up our loins, call for our dogs, and set out to partake of it all in our own way.

Sonny and I are trudging through the dark toward a small pothole located so far out on the prairie that it is almost possible to pretend that the last century of human encroachment upon the Great Plains never took place.

It is cool and still, with just enough compromise in the darkness along the eastern edge of the sky to let you know where the sun plans to come up later. On larger water the lack of wind would be a liability, but here it scarcely matters. There is no place for the ducks to raft up and those that move are not going to depend on any encouragement from the wind.

Sonny is exploring eagerly after his long ride through the darkness. It is the smell of the place that he seems hungry for after the confinement of the truck, and now he is determined to inhale all of it at once. His excitement is so contagious that it almost makes me want to pee on the tires myself. As we walk through the edge of night toward the blind, he enjoys such a great chorus of odors in the grass that I actually feel left out. I find myself wondering why nature has let us evolve beyond the mammalian sense of smell to which we seem entitled. Just as I start to feel sorry for myself, the dog circles back as if to assure me that he will share whatever his own nose happens to find. While we cannot do anything about the olfactory shortcomings of our species, we can compensate for this deficiency by spending as much time outdoors as possible in the company of hunting dogs.

We crest a little rise and drop down toward the empty spot in the grass where the water lies. A broad swath of reeds skirts the edge of the pond and we work our way noisily through it toward the blind, a simple affair of chicken wire with reeds woven through the mesh, hung from a quadrangle of old fenceposts. The blind contains a seat for my own comfort and an upended wooden crate so that the dog won't have to stand in the water unless he wants to, which he will. The blind's only real luxury is a wooden plank floor that I nailed together on the gate of the pickup and put in place before the season. It is not possible to swing a shotgun smoothly if your feet are locked into an awkward position by mud, and the sturdy planks underfoot are meant to let me move freely when the time comes.

The dog begins a slow, snuffling exploration of the reeds nearby as I rest the shotgun on the seat and carry the decoy bag out into the open water. The science of decoying waterfowl is largely lost in small potholes like this one. There is no need for large spreads to attract birds or elaborate patterns to channel their final approach. I wade along in a broad semi-circle, dropping a dozen blocks as I go. Each hits the water with a soft plop and settles at once into the inertia of decoys deprived of wind. The final result is a static display of silhouettes on reflected light. However uninspiring the spread, the voice of experience assures me that it will do.

Inside the blind, there is nothing to do but load the gun and sit and wait. I am better at this than the dog, who fidgets and frets as if something needs to be done in order to make things happen. Nothing does, of course, and coming to terms with this simple fact is a measure of maturity as a hunter. The dog is young; I can remember how he feels. I used to fidget and fret too, in duck blinds and whitetail stands and dozens of other situations where blending in and holding still were all that was really required to do it right. Now there has been a transition of sorts that is only related in part to shooting things. The fact is that I no longer regard holding still and waiting quietly as a waste of time.

There are real colors in the eastern sky now and the glassy water in front of the blind has caught them. A muskrat's leisurely progress etches an expanding pink "v" across the last obscure corners of the pond. Behind the blind, a marsh hawk begins a methodical exploration of the reeds from the air. In all my years of this, I have only seen a raptor hit my decoys once, but I always expect it to happen again. As the hawk works its way closer, I tense myself for what seems like an inevitable confrontation between predator and prey, but the bird passes by overhead without giving the decoys a second look. There is just enough color in the air to mark the hawk as a female by her brown plumage. Then she disappears behind me, hunting in her own way as I hunt on in mine. The pothole seems to have no difficulty accommodating us both.

Few good things in life arrive as dependably as shooting light, which is now spreading across the sky as the last of the stars dissolve overhead. It is time to start thinking like a hunter. A dozen black dots appear just to the left of the sunrise and I shift involuntarily in their direction before realizing that they are only redwings. "Shitbirds," I whisper to the dog, intending no real offense. The term is part of our own duck-blind vernacular, and it applies to all Unidentified Feathered Objects other than ducks. I happen to love redwings; they are simply not what I have come for today. Sonny responds by licking my face, reminding me once again that there is no established means of offending a Labrador retriever during the course of a hunt.

Then, suddenly, wings are tearing through the air. The ducks have come in from the dark side of the sky and it takes a moment for my eyes to pick them from its depths. There are four of them descending on a steep final approach with their wings locked and motionless. Their delicate outlines and the gray hues revealed by the light from the sunrise are enough to identify them as gadwalls. They all flare together as I turn and rise, and the rest occurs without any conscious thought whatsoever. The gun comes up behind the last duck so the barrel's own momentum will carry it forward through the second half of the double, and then it is done. I am scarcely aware of the shots themselves, but there are only two birds climbing back into the sun. The other two rest quietly on the water just beyond the decoys, waiting for the dog.

And that is how it is supposed to go. There is an odd detachment involved in the best of wingshooting, a sense of surrender that seems to escape most of the art's official commentators, so that one must look elsewhere for accurate descriptions. In *L'Etranger*, Camus deliberately employs a passive construction to describe the shooting on the beach. While his intention is to convey moral ambiguity, he also manages to suggest how good shots take place. In *Zen in the Art of Archery*, Herrigel's master compares the correct release of the bowstring to a snow-laden pine bough springing upward once its burden melts and falls to the ground. No one does anything. The point is simply to put oneself in a position from which events can take place. While invoking Zen imagery to describe good wingshooting technique may be stretching things a bit, the more mental clutter you have in progress when you shoot, the less likely you will be to hit what you're shooting at. And there lie two gadwalls to illustrate the point.

Few arguments for a steady dog speak with quite the authority of crowded quarters in a rickety duck blind. This morning, the pent-up excitement is just too much for an eager young dog, and Sonny is off his seat and over the front wall of the blind in a geyser of pond water before I can stop him. Both ducks are stone dead right in front of us, so there isn't anything dramatic about the retrieves. I reload, check the sky, and settle back to watch.

Sonny is whining eagerly as he swims, a certain measure of his own intensity. He has pushed a small wall of water up in front of him as he goes and when he slows down to snarf up the first duck, it spills away across the pond like a tidal wave. He is two-years old now, the color of corn husks, and pleasantly crazy. He has his own way of doing things, a trait that makes him unsuited for field trials but perfectly at home in my kennel. If called upon to do so, he will smash through ice or dive into the thorniest cover without asking anything in return other than the possibility of a bird to retrieve. Compared to such heroics, fetching the pair of gadwalls looks like bobbing for apples, but it is a pleasure to watch him anyway.

He is nearly back with the second duck when the teal appear. There is an hysterical quality to their flight across the far end of the pond, as if they are utterly unsure of their own intentions or of their relationship to one another. The little flock expands and contracts on fluttery wings as I urge Sonny back into the blind and get myself anointed with pond water once again for my trouble. None of this matters to the teal, who seem bound and determined to fly right down our throats no matter what we do to discourage them. The birds flare when they are still out of range, but we continue to track them with our eyes, since teal often do strange things when you least expect it. Sure enough—as the rest of the flock retreats into the sunrise, one bird peels away and circles back over the decoys as if daring me to shoot it, and I do.

The dog work is still routine, although you would never think so by watching Sonny himself, who surges through the retrieve as if it were the culmination of a life's work. The teal arrives delicate and unruffled, with scarcely a feather misplaced. There must be practical reasons for teal to be so beautiful, but I prefer not to worry about them. Looking at the bird is enough. The white facial crescent and the wing's delicate blue are not improved by the naturalist's compulsion to explain. With the teal beside me on the bench, my abbreviated modern limit is complete.

There are all sorts of pressures afoot these days to frame the death of game in cocktail party terms, that sometimes wind up leaving us to suggest that we kill birds in order to keep them from starving, or something equally ridiculous. There is nothing wrong with all that as far as it goes, but really...

For the record, I did appreciate the sunrise this morning, and I do look forward to tearing into these birds at the table, but above all I am here right now because it is fun to shoot ducks with a shotgun. I enjoy tracking the birds against the sky and following their progress toward the decoys. I enjoy the smooth flow of coordination between hand and eye that defines each shot. I enjoy sharing the dog's enthusiasm for each retrieve. These are all experiences that bring meaning and value to my life, and my presence here this morning requires no further explanation.

With the spell of dawn washed away by the morning sun at last, it is time to pack up and move on. Duck hunts like this are best taken in small doses; ask too much and you may strain the limits of the genre. It is perhaps worth noting how many conventions of waterfowling we did without this morning. There were no waves of mallards or undulating lines of divers, no elaborate blinds or vast spreads of decoys, no batteries of guns or complex interactions with the dog. And yet we seem to have gotten along just fine out here, alone with the ducks and the simple, reassuring feel of the place.

As I reposition the decoy bag on my shoulder and set off through the sagebrush toward the truck, I leave feeling that I have come to terms with the pond and its inhabitants. It all comes down to a matter of intimacy, of trading the flavor of the epic for something you can personally befriend. Such are the pleasures of time spent on small waters, pleasures that cannot be measured in terms of bag limits and throbbing shoulders and ringing ears.

But they can still be pleasure enough for those who take the time to seek out and enjoy them.

Prairie Hat Trick

Birds have been part of my life as long as I can remember. At first I liked to draw them (badly) and to identify them, which explains the penciled life list in the dog-eared version of Peterson's classic Field Guide that I have owned longer than any other volume in my library. When I grew big enough to shoulder a shotgun around age nine, I also discovered that I liked to shoot them, at least the ones that came into the decoys at dawn and held for the family bird dogs in the thickets around our rural home in upstate New York. My notion of American geography was firmly grounded in the plates of my Field Guide, and none was more compelling than the one that showed all those western gamebirds. Growing up in the middle of grouse and woodcock cover, it was difficult to imagine open country capable of supporting such species, much less the wildlife that actually inhabited it.

As a young man, I was fortunate enough to do just what Horace Greeley once advised all young men to do: I went west. Once I made my home on the prairie, it was hard to imagine wanting to live anywhere else. I tried once, but even Alaska wasn't enough to hold me. There were bears and sheep and salmon all right, but there just weren't enough gamebirds to keep the dogs and me happy forever.

There sure were back on the prairie, though. I once calculated that, in theory, one could legally harvest over twenty different species of gamebirds here in one day. Of course that was in the pre-drought era of tenpoint pintails and teal, but still. If one were willing to begin the day at dawn in a goose pit and hunt continually along creek bottoms and coulees and finally uphill into the mountain grouse cover, one could account for a legal limit that might embarrass Lord Ripon. That wasn't the point of course; aggregate weight of bag was never the reason I was out there. But it was still marvelously overwhelming for a kid who had grown up with the notion that variety meant having a woodcock to hang on the back porch with the ruffed grouse at the end of the day.

When it comes to gamebirds that truly define prairie bird hunting, however, you can narrow that broad list quickly. Forget the waterfowl. There is good duck and goose shooting to be had here, but you can do it elsewhere just as well. Forget the mountain grouse—the ruffs, the Franklin's, and the blues. They are boreal species that belong in a vertically oriented landscape rather than the broad open spaces that define the plains. And if you mean to be a purist, you can forget the pheasants as well, a glamour species that somehow can't stop reminding me that it doesn't really belong here in spite of its genuine appeal on the wing.

Which brings us down to three, one import and two native sons. They are the sharptail, the sage hen, and the Hun, and taken together they help to define not just a style of hunting, but the state of mind that only the prairie can afford.

The word "coulee" is derived from the French verb *couler*, to flow. There are coulees all over America of course, but only here on the prairie are these terrain features known by this highly regional term. It is hard to imagine just how the French got themselves involved in this, just as it is hard to imagine much of anything flowing in this arid country. Yet some fluid force obviously carved this one out of the prairie around us, winding elegantly around an imaginary fall line in the process. Whatever one chooses to call them, these deep, stately gouges on the face of the earth define prairie bird habitat in its native state.

From the head of this one we can study the country falling away before us as it stretches toward a distant horizon. This is no place for an agoraphobic. There is just no end to the land in front of us or the sky overhead.

The classroom for this morning's teaching exercise lies down there. I have chosen this spot deliberately. There is no wheat stubble to concentrate the sharptails artificially, no alfalfa to draw the sage hens forth at first light. Except for an occasional earthen dam off in the distance and the contrail above, the view from the head of this coulee hasn't changed a hell of a lot since Lewis and Clark passed by just north of us in 1805.

Joe is the newcomer here and I know what he's thinking. He's thinking that we could walk around out there until we die of thirst and the dogs drop from exhaustion. He just can't get the phrase "needle in a haystack" out of his mind. To the untrained eye, the countless miles of empty country stretching before us look less like prime wildlife habitat than a vast, windswept expanse of rock and sage and nothingness.

Sensing his discomfort, I try to show him what he cannot see. "Look at how the sage deepens there in the broad bottom that our coulee runs into," I explain. "That's where the sage hens will be. And see those clumps of brush on the shady side of the next coulee? That's buffalo berry, and every sharptail around will be holed up in it during the heat of the day. The Hun cover is everything in between." He still looks skeptical, but I know of no clearer way to explain this than to load the guns and turn the dog loose and walk him through it.

The point is this: there is order down there. There are gamebirds to go around. Nothingness my ass.

Hungarian partridge have a lot in common with the immigrant farmers who first settled this part of the prairie. Both arrived here from the Old World right after the turn of the century, struggled mightily to establish themselves, and survived by virtue of sheer determination. Whereas the farmers arrived from our own east coast, the Huns took a more circuitous route, migrating south under their own power from Canada where they were first introduced to the demands of the New World.

While the Hun is the only alien member of our subject trio, it's hard to begrudge its foreign origins. In contrast to pheasants and chukars, which usually look overdressed and vaguely out of place here, Huns leave you with the feeling that they might be natives themselves. Their browns and grays are the colors of the prairie, as evidenced by their ability to hide by the dozens in plain sight on open ground, and they are perhaps the most widely dispersed species of the lot.

Of course my own admiration for Huns may be biased by the fact that they are the only gamebird out here that poses much technical challenge for the experienced wingshooter. A typical Hun rise is less a flush than a detonation, delivered with a quickness that always leaves you just a little bit jumpy no matter how many times you've been through it. Their flight is swift and direct, and their flushing habits are more likely than those of any other prairie species to give you the crossing shots and overheads that experienced gunners live for. If you like to eat Huns as much as I do, you'll just have to learn to track the sound of the rise without thinking and swing the muzzle of your gun as fast as you can.

The notion of Hun cover is something of an oxymoron, for they are above all else birds of sparse tastes. You might find anything from porcupines to thirty-inch mule deer down there in the thick stuff at the bottom of the coulee, but there probably won't be any Huns at all unless we put them there. Here on the shoulders of the terrain it is another matter. "I know it doesn't look like much," I admit to Joe, "but the skinny cover is where the Huns will be. Trust me."

I have a metal snap on the front of my game vest that needs a drop of oil. The fine, high-pitched squeak it emits as I walk is a dead ringer for the sound a flock of Huns would make on the rise. No one but another prairie bird hunter would even notice it. However, years of Hun rises have conditioned me to jump when I hear that squeak, to mark and track and swing, and so the sound that no one else would notice is driving me crazy. I've had to make myself tune it out as we move along through the grass and sage, and that is why I'm a bit slow on the draw when the birds flush at last.

For the bowhunter, the essential mental exercise is picking a spot; for the Hun shooter it is picking a Hun, at least on the first rise. There are a dozen birds in this covey flushing as one, and even after all these years it is an easy matter to shoot at the whole, tightly bunched flock. I isolate and drop a trailer with my first shot but yield to indecision with the second barrel, proving once again just what an unlikely amount of air there is between those sets of whirring wings. Joe probably did much the same thing, although he may not have recognized the mistake. At least that is the most likely explanation for the fact that Sky has only one bird to present us despite four empties on the ground.

I have marked the covey down in a patch of wild roses half a coulee away. Landmarks committed to memory, it is time to cover some ground. We are both panting as loudly as the dog by the time we climb down and up again. The ground cover is only calf high, but it is thick and tenacious and this time the birds will hold. A previously flushed covey of Huns is one of the few quarries here on the prairie that sometimes makes me long for a pointer. Once again my inelegant but profoundly utilitarian Lab will just have to do.

Gunstocks upon our hips, we bracket the roses and I urge the dog forward from my side. This time everyone has read the script. Wings whir as two choose Joe's direction and two choose mine, and then there is nothing to do but fumble in the attempt to reload as the rest take to the air in all directions. When it is done, we have a Hun dinner, the dog has some retrieves to complete, and the covey has enough brood stock left to carry it through another year. Talk about happy endings.

We flush one more covey of Huns on the way down to the bottom, but they are wild and crazy, offering no shot on the rise and riding the breeze so far across the shimmering prairie that we cannot even mark them down. No matter; we can spend all afternoon chasing Huns if we wish, and we probably will.

The sage has risen around us. At the bottom of the coulee, it is tall enough to provide some shade from the September sun overhead and the leaves are still green and succulent even after the long dry season behind us. It all has to do with water, the resource hidden somewhere beneath the arid layers of soil underfoot. *Couler*; the French had it right after all.

Suddenly Sky takes on that focused look appreciated only by those who hunt regularly with flushing retrievers. Nose to the ground, he disappears into the cover and then the air is alive with wings once again. The birds are sage hens, and they stagger the rise conveniently, launching themselves from the cover in singles and pairs for half a minute before the whole flock cuts loose. After the speed and precision of the Huns' flush, these wingbeats seem ponderous and clumsy and the birds themselves appear to be the size of turkeys. Even the freshening tailwind cannot turn them into difficult targets. We each manage an authoritative, drop-dead double on the early risers, and this time I don't even try to feed the double another pair of shells as the stragglers take to the air.

Sky is taking his time even though all four falls were close and the birds fell like stones. Sage hens don't seem to smell much, and in the rising heat it takes Sky awhile to connect in spite of his years of experience at this sort of thing. In hand at last, the first of the birds feels huge in comparison to the Huns. It looks like sage and smells like sage, and by the time we each have a pair of them inside our game vests it feels as if we are carrying part of the prairie away with us as we head up out of the bottom toward the brush.

Sharptails inhabit more concise cover than other prairie gamebirds, although that doesn't necessarily mean you can find them without doing some walking. In open country, it usually makes sense to hunt terrain and habitat features that tend to concentrate game, and so it is time to introduce Joe to the silver buffalo berry, a.k.a. devil's willow for reasons that will soon become apparent.

"Don't even think about going in there," I tell Joe. Buffalo berry leaves are the lushest vegetation around and the shade beneath them seems cool and inviting, but I know all about those thorns even if he doesn't. That's why a grouse roosted in those bushes is safe from just about anything, except a determined flushing retriever.

I tell Joe to move around to the downhill side of the cover and get out where he can see and swing his shotgun. Back when we were working out the Hun covey, he kept asking me why I have nothing but Labs when a Brittany or a pointer would be so civilized and stylish. The dogs and the buffalo berry are about to illustrate my reply.

Of course not all Labs will work this kind of cover, either. Through a combination of nature, nurture, and luck, I have developed a kennel full of shock troops that hunt first and ask questions later. Don't ask me how they get through the stuff. That's their job and their problem. All we have to do is show our appreciation by hitting what they flush.

The first cluster of bushes yields two young mule deer bucks that just about run over me as they erupt from the uphill side of the cover and head for the nearest horizon. The second produces a great horned owl and the third is just plain empty. Joe declines my suggestion that we take a lunch break, and I admire his determination. He is beginning to hunt like a believer, and this kind of hunting is ultimately grounded in belief.

The next brush patch looks just like all the rest but the results of the dog's intrusion could not be more different. Suddenly the bushes are shaking with the percussion of wings. The first bird rockets out Joe's side. Uncertain of his target, he lets it sail on by.

"Chicken!" I yell, but that doesn't advance the cause much. They aren't prairie chickens, of course, but sharptails. We just call them chickens here, a colloquialism I have not yet had an opportunity to explain to Joe. Sensing his continued indecision as the next birds clear the bushes, I become less ambivalent. "*Shoot, dammit!*" I yell at the top of my lungs, and he does just that, completing his prairie hat trick in the process, a minor milestone most American gunners cannot even imagine.

Congratulations would seem to be in order.

L et me come right out and say it: The prairie may be our nation's least appreciated ecosystem. The country here is a public relations nightmare. Its pleasures are subtle and it does not photograph well. Most tourists hurry right across it going one way or the other without stopping for anything except gas. For selfish reasons, that's just fine with me. In fact, solitude is one of the reasons I love living here.

For I do love living here, and probably would even if it weren't for shotguns and generous limits and dogs that hunt as if there were no tomorrow. The prairie grows on certain people after a while and I guess I'm one of them. It has to do with sagebrush and sunsets and antelope. If a person stays out here long enough, anyone can develop an appreciation for jackrabbits and mud and dust, for blistering summer days and catfish streams and 7-Up in his whiskey after a hard day in the field.

After all of that, learning to love the bird hunting ought to be easy.

The Bird That Lives Straight Up

The Grande Ronde River coils its way through the remote southeastern corner of Washington State like a rattler poised to strike. This is arid country, since the Cascades have already caught the moisture pouring in from the cold North Pacific and kept it for themselves. The climate next to the Idaho border is nothing like that of the state's notoriously wet western half. One gets the feeling that moisture is worth something out here.

It takes a lot of work to make a river in country like this, but one look at the Grande Ronde lets you know that it is up to the task. Viewed from an airplane, the coulees and canyons of the Grande Ronde look like a scar on the face of the land around it. The tumbling current has carved a place for itself through thousands of feet of rock, and the terrain seems to accept the river's presence with the greatest reluctance.

When I was growing up in Washington, we regularly enjoyed the Grande Ronde's fine, largely unappreciated run of fall steelhead. The fall steelhead run coincided with the early bird season, however, and we knew the steep and inhospitable terrain surrounding the river as home to a species that might serve as the very definition of wingshooting to those who appreciate a challenge.

This is chukar country, and no gamebird on the continent asks quite as much of those who would pursue it.

I was alone at the oars of the drift boat with no company other than Bits, the dog. It was hard to move downstream—the pool had been generous, producing two bright fish that did everything you could ask six-pound steelhead to do. The sun had risen high enough at last to shine into the canyon and the warm Indian summer day finally felt as if it meant business. I could imagine snakes starting to stir on the sidehills as the rocks warmed, and reminded myself to watch for them when it came time to start climbing.

My father and a friend were somewhere ahead of me downriver in another boat, but they seemed as far away as the tumultuous world beyond the canyon's rims. There was no one to discuss strategy with except Bits, and I knew what he wanted to do. As if to punctuate my choice of options, a chorus of feeding calls from a flock of chukars spilled down the canyon walls, and even though it was difficult to localize the source of the sound, there was finally nothing left to do but beach the boat, uncase the shotgun, and start up through the rocks.

The terrain was steep but manageable for the first hundred yards, and as the gentle sound of the river receded behind me, I could hear birds calling even more distinctly from the cliffs overhead. The dog looked eager but I asked him to stay close to me and he did, for his eagerness was tempered by age and wisdom. Mine, however, was not, and as the ground underfoot gathered itself for its climb toward the sky, I tightened my grip on the shotgun and climbed right along with it.

It is almost a shame to carry a good double into terrain like this. In years of hunting rough country for everything from grouse to mountain goats, I have damaged firearms three times in falls and on two of those occasions the quarry was chukar. There are few arguments for slings on shotguns as compelling as a chukar hunt. I certainly could have used one that morning on the Grande Ronde as the pitch of the ground steepened beneath my feet until I longed to make the gun disappear and climb hand-over-hand unencumbered.

The birds kept calling like sirens somewhere up above me. The sun bore down and I began to sweat. I was young and Bits was old, but it was he that finally yearned to bound up the final outcropping to the birds, and I let him.

Bits scrambled out of sight above the next bastion of rocks, and then I heard him stop. I sensed that something was about to happen and dug my feet into the loose scree just as a chukar's high-pitched, pinging alarm call echoed down out of the cliffs. Then the bird was there, rocketing down-hill over my head at an angle so acute that it did not seem possible to swing a shotgun fast enough to keep pace with it.

But I did. (As I said, I was young then.) Imagine taking the high house station one bird on a skeet range while facing toward the house instead of away from it, all while balanced precariously on a steep, rocky slope, and you will have a good feel for this shot, which is a recurring theme in chukar hunting. I feel like a hero every time I make it. I could not follow the bird visually after the shot, but I felt its wings crumple as it sailed by overhead and heard its eerie cry extinguished, and I knew it was down there somewhere between me and the river, a problem for the dog once again.

Then more birds were rising above me. One flashed briefly into view, and I snapped off a shot with my second barrel that was even more ambitious than the first, to no avail. The simple act of reloading a double always seems to take forever under circumstances such as this, and true to form, a pair of birds flushed right in front of my face as I fumbled with the next pair of shells, and there was nothing to do but watch them depart. The last of the covey erupted just as I snapped the gun shut. Doubling on overhead chukars is about as tough a proposal as the world of wingshooting has to offer, and I was happy to settle for the front half of the attempt.

Then the air grew still once more. Bits materialized at my side and we turned to start downhill toward the two fallen birds and the welcome relief of the river. Only then did I realize how steep the slope had become on the way up. I slipped and slid and paused to unload the gun for safety's sake. The birds had tumbled far down the hillside and I worried about recovering them, but they were both quite dead and the dog sniffed them out with little difficulty. They were splendid in the hand, as always, with their barred side-feathers and scarlet bills, and it occurs to me now that I have taken few birds since that looked as beautiful.

It also occurs to me that I have taken few birds that were as much work.

Although chukar have been around the western Untied States since 1931, they have never acquired a following anything like that enjoyed by other imports such as the ringneck or the Hun. There are obvious reasons for this discrepancy. Chukar make a habit of running up the steep hills they inhabit and flying back down. Their human pursuers, on the other hand, are left to stagger up those same hills and sometimes count themselves lucky to crawl back toward sea level when the hunt is over.

Wildlife managers tried to make it otherwise. Chukars were given plenty of opportunity to set up shop in rolling terrain adjacent to the stubble fields that nurture so many other western gamebirds, introduced or otherwise. Thanks, but no thanks, said the chukars, who proceeded to head for the hills that resembled their own native Eurasian habitat. I suppose one should respect such proud instincts in this era of multi-culturalism. God knows you will respect them after a chukar hunt or two.

Wherever they were introduced, chukars seemed to gravitate naturally toward the least comfortable terrain around. Comfort is relative, however, and the birds liked their chosen cover for the very reasons people didn't—

it was steep, dry, rocky, windy, and difficult to get around in unless you
were a mule deer, a snake, or a chukar. Of course, the same qualities
largely define those western rangelands so useless to agricultural interests
that their control was ceded to the government years ago more or less by
default. Today, chukars seem to thrive on public land throughout their
range, an important consideration in this age of fee hunting and posted
signs, and one that contributes significantly to the chukar's slowly but
steadily growing popularity.

There are a number of conventional reasons the chukar should enjoy
more of a following as a gamebird than it does. Seasons and limits are
generous. Chukars provide opportunities for good dog work (sometimes).
They are a pleasure on the table, with light, delicate meat that enthusiastic
wild game cooks should be proud to serve to any company. And they are
strikingly beautiful birds as well, an absolutely impractical point that
nonetheless matters to people like me.

I find, however, that the most compelling element of the chukar's
appeal derives, not from any of these factors, but from what the bird has
to offer on the wing. Technically, gunning for most western gamebirds
becomes a matter of routine after a while, and the familiarity of noisy
pheasants and straight-away sharptails will eventually lead to complacency after enough years of experience. Chukars, on the other hand, never
seem to lose the capacity to surprise. They are always inventing new,
snappy angles and vertiginous overheads as they flush. Since they are
quick on the wing and the hunter is often balanced precariously on footing better suited to technical climbing gear than to shotguns, the end
result can be wingshooting as challenging as it is ever likely to get.

There is no free lunch, however, and in the case of the chukar the
check comes courtesy of the up-and-down nature of the world it inhabits.
To hunt chukars is to burn calories, stretch quads, strain lungs, and blister
feet. I have been on sheep hunts that involved less physical labor than a
typical day of chukar hunting. Sheep country is just about as steep, but
the pursuit of sheep at least means stopping to glass from time to time.
No such luxury awaits the chukar hunter, for whom every rise can be
measured by the number of contour lines broken.

There are limits to the number of people willing to go through all this
for a chance at a bird smaller than a ruffed grouse. Good chukar shooting
cannot be purchased; it can only be earned.

Of course for some, that is just the point.

It is December. Somewhere kids are making lists and people are singing Christmas carols and merchants are trying to figure out new and better ways to convince consumers to buy things that no one really needs. Of course, if someone would just buy me a fine double, I might not feel quite so distanced from all of these goings-on.

Right now, I feel remarkably detached from all of that seasonal frenzy. Alone except for my friend Joe Kelly and our two dogs, I am standing (barely) on a steep, barren sidehill somewhere in the breaks of the Columbia River. The breeze has freshened and it is blowing too hard to ignore. My Lab is at heel. Joe and his shorthair are scrambling along the same sidehill somewhere above us. The sky is cold and gray and the winter air presses in heartlessly from all sides. The rocks underfoot are treacherous and slick, but in spite of all this we are having lots of fun, Joe and the dogs and I. Honest.

We are hunting chukars. Years have passed since that morning on the Grande Ronde. I have moved to Alaska and I miss upland birds the way I miss little else about the Lower 48. I still remember the chukars, and how they flush overhead and make you swing your shotgun faster than you could ever imagine swinging it before. When Alaska's long winter nights settled in around me this year, I thought about visiting Joe and the birds in eastern Washington, and then before I could start counting the reasons to change my mind, I did just that.

It is our first morning. There is still some spring in my legs left over from Alaska's hunting season, but not nearly enough. We have started up a long, rocky slope that has grown steeper and steeper as we climbed, and now we are working parallel contour lines around the face of the hill into the most rugged country yet. We have an important ally working with us today, however—snow. The wet, white stuff settling in around the rocks promises to slow the birds down on the ground and keep them within shotgun range when they flush. The snow comes with its own price though, and we pay it with each uncertain step. Both of us have fallen several times already, and while my shotgun has not been bruised I cannot say the same for my backside.

Joe is out of sight above me when he cries "*Bird!*" and the air is suddenly alive with chukar noises. I turn and balance myself against the hillside and then the first of them appears—a quick, tight arc of motion silhouetted against the winter sky. The shotgun seems to swing on its own; the shot itself is pure instinct. The bird crumples at the gun's muffled report, and Sky is off downhill in a great, bounding commotion of a retrieve.

Moments such as this make me appreciate the Lab. Many would argue against this choice of breeds for chukar hunting. While nothing can turn a chukar hunt around with quite the authority of an experienced pointer, the retrieving breeds have a place in this game as well. A bird that falls forty yards horizontally may wind up a quarter-mile away before all that gravity and vertical terrain are through with it, and if that doesn't sound like a job for a dog with great marking ability and enthusiasm for the retrieve, I can't imagine one that does.

Sky is experienced enough that I can forget about him and the downed bird and concentrate on what is happening on the hill above me. I hear Joe shoot twice and whistle at his own dog. A pair of birds rockets by at the edge of my range and I miss, unable to get the muzzle out in front of them where it belongs. Cold fingers fumble with more shells. Joe shoots again, and then I hear the explosive cry of chukars on the wing coming from his direction. For a moment I can imagine that I am participating in some colonial parody of a European driven shoot, and then the birds are there, cutting semicircles through the air overhead at laughable angles. I snap one shot off and then they are by me, and nothing but the feel of things gone right remains to let me know that I have killed the bird.

It's all dog work now. Joe's whistle trills above me as Sky scrambles up the hill with the first dead bird. I have no idea where the second one fell and neither does he, so I must reproduce the shot and reconstruct the trajectory and leave the rest to the Lab's nose, which fortunately proves up to the task.

Joe appears on top of a rock outcropping and we compare notes by shouting back and forth at each other. He has downed a pair of birds and collected them both, so there is no need for me to climb up the hill with Sky, for which I am thankful.

Overhead, the sun is struggling through the last of the ground fog. Light sparkles suddenly from the snow, and the hills open up ahead of us like a stairway lined with crystal chandeliers. There will be more birds up there, and we have nowhere else to go but after them. The dog is eager; I, at least, am willing.

My legs gather beneath me and we set off once more into the world of the bird that lives straight up.

Brown Bombers,
Purple Sage

Even on an ordinary morning, a prairie sunrise can break your heart. Dawn on the prairie can make a photographer call for a light meter, a writer for a notebook, a hunter for a dog and gun. If you happen to be all three, you just hope that you never run out of excuses to be there.

Sometimes the excuse is a fifteen-inch antelope and sometimes it is a spread of decoys on some remote pothole. Today it is sage hens, and when the sunrise finally turns to shooting light, it is time to let Sonny out of the truck and go hunting.

There is a particular pleasure to be derived from introducing a friend to a favorite element of the outdoor world. Acting as unofficial guide allows you to participate vicariously in the pleasures of your own original discovery, no matter how long ago it occurred. This morning, my companion is an old friend from Alaska, where the selection of upland birds runs from ptarmigan to spruce grouse with very little in between. A well-traveled hunter, he has taken his share of many western species, but he has never seen a sage hen. This morning, it is my job to arrange an introduction.

The edge of the alfalfa field where I have parked the truck is the last vestige of civilization before the wilderness. Between us and the distant horizon, there are no more crops, no roads, no farmhouses. Shotguns loaded, I heel Sonny and we set out into the sage.

There will not be a lot of how-to-shoot-a-limit advice in this chapter, but here is one genuine pearl of wisdom: sage hens love alfalfa. This is fortunate, since alfalfa is one of the few crops that will grow in sage hen country. It really wouldn't have done the birds much good to develop a taste for, say, strawberries. Fortunately for all concerned, alfalfa seems to suit their needs just fine. Sage hens will travel great distances to feed in the stuff, and if there is an alfalfa field anywhere in the area, you can expect to find them near it at first light.

We have barely started to walk along the edge of the cover when I briefly glimpse an alien shape ahead of us in the sage. The oval silhouette of a sage hen's head is one of those visual cues that doesn't register until you have had some experience with it, like the white throat patch of a bedded mule deer or the outline of an elk's leg in black timber.

"There's a covey of birds up there," I warn my friend.

"Where?" he asks.

"Right there," I explain, pointing to the ground twenty yards away.

"I don't see anything," he protests.

"I know," I reply.

The bustards of the New World, sage hens are far and away our largest gamebirds, if you don't count turkeys. When out and about feeding in flocks, they are hard to miss, but when they are hunkered down in the sage—most of the time—they display some of the continent's most effective camouflage. The experienced eye may spot a head poking out above the cover, but generally the variegate pattern of gray and brown that marks their plumage makes them all but invisible.

The dog is still at heel. We ease forward slowly into the patch of cactus and sage where I have marked the birds. Enjoying my friend's absorption in an important prairie bird hunting lesson, I watch him study the nearly barren ground in disbelief. "You're seeing things," he concludes at last.

"Watch this," I reply.

It would be a mistake to say that Sonny would rather be hunting pheasants. That implies an anthropomorphic intent that is beyond the best of dogs, which in turn is one reason they are such unfailingly good company. It is fair to point out that Sonny does not seem as excited right now as he does when we are hunting ringnecks, although I suspect this has more to do with the scenting qualities of sage hens than with some system of values on his part. Nonetheless, his sudden intensity suggests that his nose has finally picked up a whiff of something worth hunting. I urge him forward and suddenly the morning sky is full of wings.

There is an eerie quality to the sage hen's rise, much of which is auditory. They do not vocalize when they flush. There is none of the pheasant's cackle, the sharptail's chatter, the Hun's rusty-hinge squeaking. I am reminded of Alexander the Great's psychologically devastating tactic of marching his troops into battle in silence. As the birds flush before us now, there is nothing but the hollow sound of wings straining to get all that weight airborne. It sounds like a lot of work, and I am sure that from an aerodynamic perspective, it is.

Hopelessly rattled, my friend stares, finally isolates a bird from the flock, and misses. This is not an entirely unusual reaction to one's first encounter with sage hens on the wing. It's not that they're hard targets; it's just so damn unsettling when you see them flush for the first time. "Reload," I urge quickly. "There is going to be a straggler."

As indeed there is. Sonny locates the last bird and noses it into the air just as my friend snaps the over-and-under closed. More collected now, he swings smoothly, and the bird collapses at the sound of the shot and crashes to the ground with an audible thud.

Moments later, Sonny delivers the bird to my hand. A mature cock, it is quite a mouthful for the dog. When I accept the delivery and hand it to my friend to study, I choose not to spoil the moment by telling him that, for culinary reasons, experienced gunners deliberately select the smallest birds from each covey. Ignorance is bliss. He hefts his prize in awe, wearing the dumbstruck look of a hunter who has just walked up to his first dead moose. This single specimen weighs as much as an entire limit of most upland birds. "In all my years of hunting," he observes quietly, "I've never seen anything quite like this."

And he's right of course, for there isn't anything quite like a sage hen.

There is something wonderfully anachronistic about *Centrocerus urophaisianus*. Sage hens are not fast, agile, or particularly smart. They have succeeded as a species by adapting to sparse terrain that does-n't seem to interest much of anybody else. They cope well with drought, lean food supplies, and cold winters. They do not benefit from human intrusion the way many western gamebird species do. Whenever I encounter them, I am subliminally reminded of Lewis and Clark, covered wagons, and Charlie Russell paintings, for those terms define the century to which the sage hen belongs.

Hunting sage hens can be a puzzling affair. A recounting of my own first sage hen hunt, which took place over twenty years ago, serves to illustrate some of the problems. It was my first season on the prairie. Two local acquaintances asked if I wanted to go bird hunting with them, an offer I couldn't refuse. The following morning we rose in the dark and drove for hours into the sage brush wilderness north of Fort Peck Lake. Finally the driver stopped in a place that looked pretty much like every-thing else we had driven through for the last twenty miles. "Great place for sage hens," he assured me.

"By God," his partner said from the aptly named shotgun seat, "there's some now!"

The two of them grabbed their guns and scrambled from the truck as the prairie began to spew birds in unbelievable numbers. A few minutes later, the back of the pickup was ankle deep in what could be charitably described as our limit of sage hens. "Great hunt," I remember someone saying as we rattled back toward the world of paved roads and I nodded off to sleep again.

It was not the sort of first impression that inspires confidence.

If the central feature of the American experience is indeed space, this principle is seldom demonstrated more completely than in sage hen coun-try. Therein lies part of the problem. To the casual observer, the prairie can seem intimidating—a vast, monotonous sea gone dry, where every-thing is flat and open and overwhelming. In the end, there is just so much of it. The mere thought of looking for something out there can cause distress. Couple this sense of futility with the fact that it is possible to drive a four-wheel drive vehicle almost anywhere sage hens live, and it's easy to see how so many sage hen hunts wind up missing the point.

The prairie's apparent sameness from one corner to another is of course an illusion. The prairie is no more uniform than a bonefish flat or a duck marsh. Study the terrain carefully and you will notice folds and wrinkles in its surface. Wherever these contours allow the gathering of an extra dash of moisture now and then, the cover will be denser, the sage more lush and green. In time, you will realize that the birds will be there, and not in the other ninety-nine percent of the country, and then you can begin to hunt them in earnest.

It is hard to know just what to call sage hens. They seem to lack the intuitive nicknames enjoyed by most other gamebird species. Some local hunters call them "brown bombers," a term that rings true in an oddball sort of way, since it so economically describes the bird in flight. The sage hen's wings are designed for lift, rather than speed, agility, or endurance. Sage hens lumber into the air and drone as they fly. If you can imagine Huns as Messerschmidts, sage hens are quite logically B-17s.

That lack of punch on the wing explains my one reservation about sage hens as gamebirds—they are just a bit too easy. An experienced wingshooter can quite reasonably expect to get through a typical season without missing one. I can't say with a straight face that I never miss sage hens anymore, but when I do it is usually accompanied by a "how-the-hell-did-you-do-that?" shake of the head. True, late season birds tend to gather in large, wary bunches just like sharptails and they can be significantly tougher than their September counterparts, but even then challenging gunning is not a large part of the sage hen's appeal.

On the other hand, the very characteristics that make the sage hen a bit too easy for the veteran—slow, purposeful flight; close, controlled shots at tightly holding birds—also make the brown bomber ideal for beginners. At our house, an annual September sage hen hunt has been a family tradition for years, as my kids joined legions of youngsters introduced to the pleasure of the shotgun courtesy of this accommodating species.

A few technical notes for those who, like my Alaskan friend, are intrigued by sage hens without ever having seen one:

Despite their size, they are not difficult birds to bring down. Any choke and load appropriate for pheasants is perfectly adequate. The improved cylinder and modified over-and-under that I use on grouse and Huns has served me well for years and the kids in our crew do just fine with .410s.

Sage hens don't offer particularly exciting dog work. Early in the season, hot prairie weather often leads to poor scenting conditions. Gun dogs seem to have a lot of difficulty with sage hens anyway, possibly because they smell so much like the sage in which they reside. While downed birds seldom run, a good retriever is still useful. I seldom hunt anything that flies without a Lab at my side, and the sage hen is no exception. Nonetheless, it is not utterly unreasonable to hunt sage hens without a dog, a statement I cannot make about any other western gamebird. Except for retrieves, the main function of my own Labs on sage hen hunts is to keep me company out in the middle of nowhere.

No discussion of the sage hen is complete without reference to its quality on the table, where its reputation has suffered for years. Yes, older birds can be tough, and yes, they are all more vividly flavored than some other species. Young birds of the year are usually delicious, however, which is why those in the know deliberately aim for them. With a bit of imagination even their older relatives can be turned into succulent fare. If all this suggests the biased opinion of one who has prepared and eaten with gusto his share of sage hen enchilladas, Szechuan sage hen, sage hen Parmesan, and whatnot, rest assured that your intuitions are correct.

And so with all those warm feelings toward the sage hen on the record, could I hunt them day in and day out for the rest of my life the way I could hunt sheep or whitetails, ptarmigan or pintails? No, I could not. In fact, I rarely take more than a pair or two a season now, and then usually when I am in the company of visitors or my kids. Despite the place they occupy in my heart, I am more likely to hunt sage hens with my longbow or my camera than with my double and all the serious intentions it implies.

It is worth noting that man has not always been kind to the sage hen. At the turn of the century, populations were dangerously low throughout the West. The presence of huntable numbers of sage hens on the prairie today is yet another testimonial to the principles of sound game management. Allowing for the vagaries of weather and habitat conditions, sage hen numbers are now generally stable throughout much of their historic range.

Such developments, however, can lead to ill-advised complacency. There will always be people interested in turning the prairie into something else, which usually means something more lucrative for them. Since the economy of the Great Plains is chronically depressed and not much of anyone lives out here but a few ranchers, romantics, and fools, it seems logical to assume that no one should complain about progressive ideas like turning the prairie into a bombing range or toxic waste dump.

Well, I am complaining. I am doing so on behalf of those ranchers, romantics, and fools; the sage hens, antelope, and mule deer; and, while we're at it, myself (no matter which of the three previously mentioned categories of people you might imagine to include me).

It is not possible to fully appreciate any game species outside the context of its habitat or its history. Therein lies the real allure of a bird that flies as if it has water in its fuel tanks and tastes as if it had a collision with the spice cabinet on the way to the kitchen. The sage hen is a relic from an era when a transcontinental America was simply an idea, just as it is now an excuse to be out in the prairie when the sun comes up.

Those are reasons enough to care about the brown bomber and the places it lives, no matter what it does or does not have to offer on the wing.

The Essentials
of Waterfowling

Some years back I subscribed to a newsletter devoted to the subject of hunting ducks. This publication may or may not still be in existence. The first issue I received was devoted to exploring the definition of a "world class" duck hunt. There were several first-person descriptions of hunts in countries unfettered by the concept of limits, with cases of shells shot, multiple species taken, and guides groaning under the weight of the bag at the end of the day. I did not renew my subscription.

I have participated in the rituals of the duck blind since early childhood. During my medical internship twenty years ago, hospital duties kept me from spending the opening morning of duck season in the field for the first time in memory and the sense of loss was almost unbearable. (Of course I did leave work that evening, drive to the countryside outside of Montreal, spend the night in an unsuspecting farmer's cornfield, and...well, that's another story.) At any rate, subsequent years of experience have taught me that the best way to get a fix on outdoor sport is to refine, rather than expand, the scope of its discussion. Now it seems to be precise moments rather than weighty bags that transform my sense of time in the field. Nowhere is this principle more evident than in the duck blind, where a decade of drought has changed all the rules of the game and the pleasures are less likely to come from furious shooting than from a few essential images, distilled to clarity and rendered with the simplicity of a single brush stroke. Consider a few of my own favorites.

The Water Entry

There is no practical reason why retrievers should launch themselves over the water like cruise missiles. They could just trot down the bank instead, extend a toe, and lower themselves in like matrons at a public beach. You would probably have just as many ducks in the game bag at the end of the morning.

So why get so excited about a wet dog lunging wildly into a pond? If you have to ask, you have either never seen it done right, or I probably cannot help you.

A heart-stopping water entry invokes that sense of passion alluded to in an earlier chapter, the feeling that may be our culture's answer to the bullfight. For an instant, the animal's judgment is utterly suspended as it surrenders to its instincts without regard for the consequences. Coming from our own structured world, we need this sort of thing from time to time, even if we have to experience it by proxy through our dogs.

If you are hunting with a Lab, much of this will be done for you, and devotion doesn't get any more sincere, especially if the body of water in question is full of ice. Of course, if you are hunting with a Chessie, the dog will be doing it all for himself, but you are still welcome to watch. Either way, the water entry, properly performed, can be viewed as both a necessary and sufficient reason to be there.

Swamp Things

I am not really a hard-core goose hunter, but I have friends who are. "Don't set up on the water!" they're always telling me. "That screws everything up. Do some scouting, find where they are feeding, and dig a pit in the field."

I know that is how you are supposed to do it, but I have a confession to make: With all due respect to my friends in the farming community, there are few places on earth as boring as the middle of a large stubble field. Even when flavored with the promise of geese, time spent there passes slowly.

Now contrast that tedium with the goings-on at your nearest wetland. We are not necessarily talking about the Great Dismal Swamp; any patch of water large enough to hold a few decoys will do. While the exact cast will change with the seasons, here is a short list of welcome distractions one can expect to encounter between summer blind-building and the end of the late season: muskrats, cattails, yellow-headed blackbirds, raccoons, low-flying marsh hawks, freshwater shrimp, foraging mink, pelicans, dragonfly husks, the cries of killdeer, great blue herons still as statues, watering antelope, sandpipers I cannot identify without my bird book, fish skeletons picked clean by scavengers, and everywhere the fecund stink of rich, primordial mud.

With all that around, who needs the geese?

Geese

I do, at least every once in a while.

In some ways, those of us who seldom hunt geese seriously are able to appreciate them more than those who hunt them all the time. When you set out a truckload of silhouettes and spend the morning supine in a goose pit, you expect to shoot geese. On the other hand, when your Thanksgiving dinner depends on the occasional lost honker dropping into your mallard decoys unannounced, the geese so taken assume special significance. The shock of their size generates excitement the same way elk do when you run into them deep in the timber when you are really hunting deer.

If you take your geese by accident rather than design, the distant cry of a lone honker can cause panic in a duck blind as cold hands reach for goose calls and magnum shells and unruly dogs are suddenly whacked into obedience. Should the bird turn and look you over and set its wings, the anticipation can become practically unbearable. You will remember such geese long after the memory of more organized and productive goose hunts has faded. So while I have great respect for my friends who take their geese deliberately, I am happy to go right on shooting them in my own helter-skelter way.

Besides, I never really liked digging goose pits.

Downwind Highballers

As a student of wingshooting, albeit an informal one, I know of nothing quite like a pair of pintails screaming by overhead with a thirty-knot wind behind them.

Never mind the romance of ducks settling into a spread of decoys. When it comes to putting a duck and a column of shot in the same place at the same time, that's kid stuff. Imagine instead that you are dealing with one or two ducks rather than a whole flock, that said ducks are going from point A to point B when they decide to give your spread the once-over, and that the same north wind that has stirred the water and flattened the reeds and sent the coots scurrying for shelter has gotten this pair of birds moving with conviction. Now you and your shotgun are faced with what can easily be called a challenge. Of course you can always let them go by and hope they come around to offer something more civilized, but most of the time you know they won't, so you won't either. Once you have made a positive identification, your cerebral cortex is best left in neutral until the shooting is over. I could burn a thousand words telling you how I approach such shots, but I doubt that would do anyone much good. So just time your rise properly, begin your swing well behind the bird as you are mounting the gun, and drive the barrel through the target faster than you ever thought possible. If you have done everything just right, with the hands and eyes obedient only to each other, the duck will shudder gently at the shot and just stop living thirty yards above the blind. Then its momentum will carry it by overhead, leaving you to hope that the dog somehow managed to mark the fall. These, too, are birds that will endure in the memory.

Orange Feet

As noted, ducks landing in decoys do not offer technically difficult shooting, a fact that only serves to make this part of the hunt contemplative and enjoyable in other ways. Most wingshooting involves active pursuit. Hunting ducks over decoys, on the other hand, is more reminiscent of fishing, in that it requires convincing the quarry to do something specific. Here, for once, is both a means and an opportunity to settle back and observe.

Convincing a flock of wary puddle ducks to set their wings and land in your lap is a form of seduction, an exercise whose appeal is celebrated in the long tradition of the decoy carver's art. One can end the affair at any time just by standing up and shouting, "Gotcha!" The shotgun itself would be almost an afterthought if ducks weren't such a pleasure on the table. As with fishing, the triumph comes more from the strike—the final measure of deception—than from bringing the fish to the net. But how does one identify this essential moment in the duck blind?

Ducks, of course, have aerodynamically efficient ways of handling their landing gear in flight. Their drag-inducing legs retract against their bellies as smoothly as a jetliner's wheels. It is almost impossible to see them when a bird is on the wing—unless the duck is committed to a landing.

And so it is the extension of the legs toward the water that finally serves to mark small triumphs in the duck blind. The appearance of the feet is often accompanied by a brief backward flurry of the wings, as if contact with the water might actually be painful. The bird will flex its neck just beyond the body while extending its head, creating an uncertain bow in its profile as it lands. When all these things happen right in front of my blind, I know that I have done just what I set out to do.

In the case of the mallard, this final commitment is made especially vivid by the brilliant orange color of the feet. Their appearance confirms success in the art of deception. In these times of restricted limits, such moments can define the reasons for getting up in the dark and thrashing around in the mud as surely as the shot itself.

Wings Overhead

It would be a shame to forget that experiences in the field are defined by the ears as well as the eyes.

Many years ago, as a kid in New York state, I spent an evening sitting alone beside a large beaver pond as darkness fell around me. Near the end of shooting light, a huge flight of migrating mallards and black ducks arrived overhead. I had never heard anything quite like the roar made by all those wings above me in the darkness. Those were the days of peak Cold War nuclear jitters and I remember thinking quite seriously that we might be under some kind of attack. When I finally did make out the ducks settling in around me through the alders, I was too awestruck to think about shooting. Even after all these years, I am hard pressed to imagine a better demonstration of natural energy.

And the sound of duck wings still moves me, especially when they are tearing by overhead in the pre-dawn darkness. That is a sound that defines anticipation and provokes anxious glances at the wristwatch, whose hands seem to be moving all too slowly toward the hour of legal shooting light. It is both a reminder of things past and a promise of things to come, and the human ear just can't do much better than that.

Canine Company

I have an ambivalent attitude toward companionship in the field. Virtually all my close friends are serious hunters, and we spend a lot of time discussing hunting and related activities, as one might imagine. And when you have lost a dog or shot an elk down in the bottom of some miserable hole, its nice to know who your friends are, as you certainly will if you make a habit of calling people at all hours of the night requesting assistance with problems of this sort. Nevertheless, solitude is one of the reasons I love the outdoors, and the notion of the hunt as a social affair has never held much appeal for me.

It's still nice to have some company when it is cold and wet and dark out there, and nothing fits the bill quite like a Labrador retriever. Personality is one driving reason behind the breed's enduring appeal. Being good company is potentially a mixed blessing, now that more and more Labs are being bred by people who neither know nor care about hunting, a fate unlikely to befall certain other breeds, such as Chesapeake Bay retrievers and blue-tick hounds. In the meanwhile, one might as well enjoy what the Lab has to offer.

When hunting upland game with flushing retrievers, you don't get to spend a lot of quality time with the dogs. They are out there in the cover for the most part, and whether you are shouting praise or curses at them, it's all still shouting in the end, and that can only go so far.

The duck blind is another matter. Duck blinds are great places to begin and end friendships, with people and dogs alike. I've hunted with dogs that seemed perfectly agreeable in larger quarters, only to find them intolerable in the confining ambience of a blind. On the other hand, the dogs that I have enjoyed most over the years have always been a pleasure even there, where the potential for a large, wet animal to become bad company is enormous.

The difference between a good blind dog and a bad one is surprisingly difficult to define, and certainly goes beyond such straightforward matters as shaking water all over you, which even the best of the lot will do from time to time. I suppose it finally comes down to a matter of attitude and the ability to convey the belief that hunting is the most important thing imaginable without being a pain in the ass about it. Of course, that happens to be pretty much the standard I hold people to as well. What a coincidence.

Crisp on the Outside

If wild ducks tasted like tuna casserole or pickled beets, my attitude toward them would hardly be the same, especially when viewed down the top of a ventilated rib. It is one of the outdoors' great bonuses that ducks are as much fun to eat as they are to shoot, which adds a whole new dimension to activities in the duck blind.

The history of duck on the table is certainly a rich one. Consider, for example, the curious case described by one Dr. Boerhaave, who in 1724 attended a Dutch naval officer who had eaten a wild duck with such gusto that he quite literally split his gullet open, an incident that allowed Boerhaave to contribute his name to the eponym for spontaneous rupture of the esophagus, even as it defined some sort of outer limit to enthusiasm for good food. It would be interesting to know how Boerhaave's patient prepared his duck.

The wild duck, like all successful life forms, is a natural marvel of design. While its flight characteristics are certainly impressive, the degree to which it has adapted to time spent on the water may be even more so. Anyone who can remember setting decoys out in a frigid pond will understand the problem at once. As warm-blooded vertebrates, ducks don't tolerate hypothermia any better than we do. Their blueprint addresses these environmental demands in several ways: the elaborate oils that coat their feathers; the layers of down with a ratio of insulation-to-weight that still exceeds what man can accomplish in the laboratory; and the dense fat that accumulates beneath the skin on surfaces likely to have contact with the water.

Fat, of course, has become a pejorative buzzword in our modern dietary vocabulary. It is not my intention to bore you with a lot of quasi-scientific rambling about the nutritional value of teal. We all have more important things to worry about. The fact remains that it is precisely that layer of fat that allows wild duck to reach its full expression on the table.

I am not writing about game cookery—if you want recipes, you will have to look somewhere else. Sauces and seasonings are irrelevant to the current discussion anyway. This is a matter of texture and natural taste. When it's done just right, a wild duck's skin should turn crisp in the oven, as that adaptive layer of fat seals the juices into the breast by magic. When you bite into a duck that has been prepared just so, you can expect an explosion of taste that will explain why skinning a duck is regarded as a crime against nature, at least in our family. That bite should also be enough to make you view with suspicion those who disdain duck on the table, the fate of Boerhaave's long dead naval officer notwithstanding.

And with that bite, I bring this brief survey of waterfowling's essential moments to a close. Your own list will probably differ from my own, as well it should. The important thing is that you have one and that you refer to it often during the course of each season, for when you do, any hunt can become world class.

It is as simple as a retriever hitting the water or a mallard's feet extended in the morning sun.

The Last September

We had nothing in common, Joe and I, but a regard for shotguns, bird dogs, and the outdoors.

When I graduated from high school in a comfortable Seattle suburb, the class pundits made the usual smug predictions about the future, as members of high school graduating classes do everywhere. You can imagine the routine: Most Likely to Succeed, Most Likely to Go to Jail, Most Likely to Lose His Hair. Had there been a category for Most Likely to Die in an Unpopular War, I probably would have had the foresight to nominate my friend Joe. At the time, of course, no one could have imagined such a thing. We had a lot to learn, and we were about to start learning sooner than any of us could have imagined.

I would not have made this hypothetical prediction because of politics or idealism—to the best of my knowledge Joe was not burdened by either. It was a matter of character. He seemed fascinated by danger even as he demonstrated a quiet disregard for its consequences. At the time, this seemed to be nothing more than another permutation on the attitudes toward life that get teenaged males in trouble. I suppose that in a less cynical age this combination of traits might even be called bravery. At any rate, there we were in a school full of kids concerned with matters that mystified us, who would eventually enjoy the distinction of growing up to become the world's first crop of yuppies. Even then, I sensed that they had it all wrong. Joe had a shotgun and a dog and so did I, and in those surroundings we needed nothing more to form the basis of an understanding.

During the first few weekends of September, when the doves were still gathered in eastern Washington, we would commandeer a car and head to the Yakima Valley, leaving our classmates to dither about homecoming parades, Corvettes, and similar hallmarks of spoiled '60s adolescence. Joe had spent his early childhood in Yakima and he knew his way around the country. By day, we would sneak into likely looking fields and shoot doves until one of four things happened:

1. We shot our limit of doves (or our liberal Huck Finn interpretation thereof);

2. We ran out of shells;

3. The owner of the field chased us out (My concept of landowner relations was in its embryonic stages at the time); or

4. It became too dark to shoot.

When condition number four was finally realized with or without dove limits, leftover ammunition, or discouragement by offended farmers, we would head for town and the cauldron of hormones that boiled over on Yakima's main drag every Saturday night. We generally fared better with the doves than we did with the girls, which was probably just as well for all concerned. When we got back to school on Monday morning, our classmates were always asking us about football games we had not attended. The news that we had been hunting often drew perplexed stares, an eerie premonition of attitudes to come. We never knew quite what to say.

The last September arrived with that certain ambivalence known only to young men who realize that they have just enjoyed their final summer vacation. I was going to college. Joe didn't know what he was doing. The doves knew what they were doing though, so we piled into Joe's folks' car and headed across the Cascades.

After the usual preliminary scouting, we found our way into a narrow field between a vast expanse of hops and an irrigation ditch. The air was full of doves. They were silhouetted sharply against the azure sky and flew with the intense wingbeat that unequivocally confirms them as game, in spite of their superficial resemblance to songbirds. We were not the only shooters to discover this bonanza, however—a half-dozen older men were strung out at regular intervals along the edge of the field. They all seemed to know each other, and they were subtly unenthusiastic about our intrusion, although no one came right out and said anything. Several of them bore elegant doubles, and well-mannered dogs sat dutifully at their feet. Silent disapproval flavored the stifling air as we walked behind the firing line, as if we had arrived underdressed at a formal wedding.

"What the hell," Joe said with an unconcerned shrug as he led the way toward an unoccupied spot along the ditch. He was never one to stand on ceremony.

Our seasoned competitors were hitting some birds, but they were missing a whole lot more. Their well-bred dogs weren't looking too sharp in the heat, either. They were panting miserably and missing their marks, and when they did make retrieves, they were obviously unhappy about the dove feathers that stuck to their tongues. None of these details escaped my attention during the long, slow walk toward our place beside the ditch.

We sat down side by side, established shooting lanes, and put our one box of shells down on the dirt between us where we both could reach it. Joe had brought no dog that year. My own brain-damaged shorthair proceeded to wallow in the mud lining the irrigation ditch, becoming at once the ugliest and the happiest dog in the field. We laughingly christened him the Mud Pig and settled into the business of trying to stay out of his way. And then the doves began to trade overhead in earnest.

Mourning doves really want to do just three things: eat, drink, and roost. While I don't have a lot to offer about the technical aspects of dove hunting, I can emphasize that the object of the game is to be between the places where they are doing any two of the three. And if you are doing your dove shooting in places like Washington and Montana, as I have done mine, it will help tremendously if you arrive at your chosen spot before the doves have all flown south to provide sport in California and Texas. On this particular September day, we had managed these simple goals to perfection.

By strange coincidence, we each experienced one of those stellar afternoons when it does not seem possible to miss a moving target with a load of shot. The doves flew straight and true as they passed by overhead, inviting one perfect exercise in geometry after another. Each one seemed to be asking us to track and swing easily along its course of flight, and that is just what we did, without making matters one bit more complicated than they needed to be. There was a ten-bird limit in effect and we played it straight, perhaps because of all the company and perhaps because that day simply marked the final passage of the occasional immature impulse to shoot more that the law allowed when our fathers weren't around to keep tabs on us. At any rate, two times ten is twenty, and there were still a couple of shells rattling around inside the box when we were through.

My filthy shorthair was having a good day, too. It took him a while to pick up all of our birds, along with a few of someone else's. As we awaited the Mud Pig's final return, I realized that the shooting all around us had stopped. Everyone was looking quietly in our direction, and the other dogs even seemed to be watching the shorthair with envy. On all those faces, human and canine alike, looks that once asked, "What is this neighborhood coming to?" had given way to expressions asking, "Who are these guys?"

I remember clearly how it ended. Joe was wearing a crazy billed cap of some kind to keep the sun out of his eyes. He stopped and doffed his hat just as Babe Ruth might have done at Yankee Stadium after a homer, and then we walked out of the field without looking back. I heard murmured discussion behind us, and no one started shooting again until we were halfway to the car. And I know this just as clearly as I know that memory: I have spent many days with a shotgun in the years since, but I cannot remember a single one that I have enjoyed more.

On the long drive back home through the mountains, I admitted that I was apprehensive about going away to college. Joe said he might join the Marines. There were all kinds of things happening in Vietnam, he said. Like what, I wanted to know? Imagine.

Back at my parents' house, I unloaded my gun and my gear and kenneled the Mud Pig before he could provoke the wrath of God, a.k.a. my mother. Then we divided the birds in the ice chest and said goodbye. We never saw each other again.

June in Alaska is a frantic time for the outdoorsman. Seasons pass quickly in the far north, and when the days lengthen and the mud finally dries out, all the latent ambitions of the long, dark winter come boiling forth, spurred by the certainty that if you don't do it now, it will soon be winter again. That June was no exception. There were kings in the river, the flying weather was good, and the bears were not yet rubbed hopelessly. With this embarrassment of riches about, I had a lot on my mind as I left work that day. Hurried and distracted, I almost drove right by the sign directing me to the mobile reconstruction of the Vietnam War Memorial.

But I didn't. Perhaps it was because of the announcement inviting me to the twentieth reunion of my high school class. Who knows how they found me? I had made no effort to leave a trail. But there had been the letter, and I opened it with all the trepidation an anti-social person typically brings to bear on such occasions. I admit feeling a grim fascination with the whole idea, but then grim fascination is the emotion locked deep inside us all that makes twenty-year reunions work in the first place. The invitation contained the usual details about the affair to be held in Seattle. It also included a somber note in memory of those members of the class known to have passed away, which is how the well-intentioned people who become class secretaries put it when they are trying to tell you that your old friends are dead. The list seemed surprisingly long to someone who still considered himself and his contemporaries young. Some of the names on the list were predictable, while others were quite unexpected. And there was Joe's, just as I had known it would be from the occasional fragments of communication I maintained with a few of my old class-mates.

And so I followed the sign, and I felt these things as I did: helpless-ness, fascination, exhilaration, dread. An odd, general sense of detach-ment from current events prevails in Alaska, and I realized how distant many of society's concerns had grown while I lived there. I was not alone before that awesome black wall, however, and it was reassuring somehow to note that everyone else seemed as edgy about the experience as I was. The search took some time, but then I found him, sixteen sim-ple letters adrift in a sea of names. Soon I was tallying events I would never have experienced if my own name had been there as well: sheep hunted, dogs buried, children fathered, women loved. I spent more time there than I thought I would, and then I left with nothing resolved. That was what hurt us all so badly in the end, that absence of resolution. There were other names I could have looked for, but I didn't have another one in me.

I drove home quietly, past the river and the airfield. The beauty of the forest around me seemed muted somehow. My attention belonged to another place and another time, when two kids paused briefly in a dusty field to show the world just what it was that they had to show.

Knuckleheads
and Wild Ringnecks

There were dozens of places we could have hunted that day and the list of possibilities read like an encyclopedia of good pheasant cover: CRP bordering golden stubble fields, river bottoms lined with willows and chokecherries, uncultivated swales full of wild roses and native grasses that can make you wonder how this country ever got by without pheasants before their introduction a hundred years ago. But the hunting season was reaching its own middle age and the prairie lay in the grips of the first hard snow of the year. The birds were going to be stacked up in the middle of the nastiest, most impenetrable escape cover they could find, and I knew just the place to look for them.

The rancher, a longtime friend, had warned me when I called the night before to confirm my standing invitation to hunt the place. It had been a wet year, he reminded me. The cover was high and thick and the creek bottoms we planned to hunt still held lots of water. One or two other local hunters had been out earlier, but they had been unable to move many birds from the heavy cover. Ray and I remained undeterred as we finalized our plans over coffee. We could have predicted everything the rancher had told me anyway. His place has always held a special appeal during the late season, and I imagined how the cattails in the creek bottom would feel brittle in the frost and what the roosters would sound like as they fought their way through them toward the sky when they flushed. There might be easier places to hunt, but today I wouldn't miss this one for the world.

During the hour's drive from my house to the ranch, the countryside around us seemed stunned, as if it was not ready yet for the changing of the seasons. The puddle ducks that had dotted the stock ponds a few days earlier were gone and the antelope along the roadside stood and stared indifferently as if they were preoccupied with the promise of winter. Finally, we turned off the county road and eased down a rutted two-track and there was the creek bottom, as devilish and defiant a patch of late season pheasant cover as one could ever imagine.

We stopped at our customary parking spot and opened the dog box in the back of the truck, and my Lab and Ray's Chessie spilled forth. The dogs were uncontainably excited. The dry snow exploded beneath their feet and hung shimmering in the sunlight as they roared around and jumped up on us enthusiastically, displaying just the sort of canine bad manners that never seem to bother me as much as I know they're supposed to. They were our secret weapons, the reason I never pay any attention when well-meaning landowners tell me that the birds have been tough lately. All the dogs wanted now was a chance to go hunting, a desire that made perfect sense to me.

As I sat down on the tailgate of the truck and struggled into my hip waders, one foot brushed against the ground by accident and contaminated my wool sock with snow. That is just the sort of trivial mishap that can aggravate you all day long. The rubber boots felt stiff and confining and I tried to talk myself right back out of them, but the voice of my own experience prevailed. I knew what was waiting down in the creek bottom and the desire to hunt in leather boots wasn't going to make the footing any drier. The cold shudder of snow in my left boot made me grimace as I stood, but finally there was nothing to do but reach for my game vest and go hunting.

After walking easily across two hundred yards of stubble, climbing down into the creek bottom felt like a descent into hell. The artificial civility of cultivation yielded at once to a murderous tangle of brush, beaver workings, and thorns in a dozen different shapes and sizes, as if all the flora there had been designed to protect the place against intrusion. Along the bottom of the draw, the partly frozen creek expanded and contracted according to the whim of the beavers. The ice was too thick to walk through and too thin to walk on, and treacherous sink holes were everywhere. It was simply no place for right-thinking people. No wonder the pheasants love it there.

Our routine felt easy and familiar, the way combat must feel to well-trained troops. One of us would take the dogs through the brush toward the apex of each curve in the creek while the other waited where the water pushed against the high bank at the outside of the bend. As the two dogs worked their way through these naturally defined segments of cover, the creek closed relentlessly on the birds running in front of them, until they had no choice but to flush. Each of us knew just where to go and just what to do without even having to discuss it, and the dogs were both veterans at this exercise.

The first bend produced a handful of hens and a lone rooster for Ray. I was the blocker on the second push, and doubled easily on the pair of ringnecks that the dogs flushed over my head. The next stretch of cover, an isolated oxbow, proved to be the honey hole. I swung on a noisy rooster that tried to cut behind me and completed my limit while Ray quickly managed an overhead double of his own. For another minute, the dogs worked pheasants against the oxbow's outside bank and nosed them into the air, until we finally collected our canine friends and sent them on the retrieves they were bred for in the first place.

"You know," Ray said as we hauled ourselves up out of the creek bottom and started back across the field toward the truck. "We could have hunted here all morning without seeing a bird if it hadn't been for the knuckleheads."

I mumbled in agreement and reached down to pull a cluster of burrs from my wool pants. The weight of the birds in the game vest felt like an apology for the creek bottom's uncivil manners. I remembered my rancher friend and the pessimism he expressed and imagined earlier hunters nibbling around the edges of the cover without benefit of experienced dogs. Beside me, the Lab was staring longingly back toward the creek as if he were sorry to have the morning end so soon.

While I have great respect for the pointing breeds, I remain a hopeless afficionado of the Labrador retriever. I love Labs; don't ask me to explain. We just seem to understand each other and to approach the world with a fundamentally similar set of priorities, an admission with which certain co-workers and an ex-wife would no doubt agree. Because I make it a point to live in places where I can hunt a lot, my kennel has to be productive. It also has to be versatile, since any given day here on the prairie might provide the opportunity to hunt everything from Huns to geese. Sure I could have Labs *and* more traditional upland bird dogs, but every place in the kennel occupied by something other than a Lab would be, well, one less Lab in my life. I told you not to ask for explanations.

These circumstances have led me to accumulate more than my share of experience with flushing retrievers, dogs that have never enjoyed the reputation they deserve in sophisticated wingshooting circles. They are all too often dismissed as dogs that couldn't make it by "real" retriever standards, or as an unsophisticated hunter's poor substitute for a properly trained pointer.

Part of the problem is historical. Flushing retrievers don't really come into their own as upland bird dogs unless they are hunting pheasants. By the time pheasants were introduced to the West, Labs and Chessies had years of American waterfowling tradition behind them. Virtually everything official concerning these popular breeds ignored their utility as upland gun dogs—everything, that is, except an appreciation of their versatility by the people who love to hunt with them.

Flushing retrievers demand their own approach to hunting upland game. Part of the problem is that lots of people just don't get it, especially those who have spent their days afield in the company of pointing breeds. A dog that flushes birds generally does little good unless the blessed event takes place within shotgun range, a need that can be addressed in different ways. You might learn to run faster than the dog, in which case you should stop wasting time in hunting boots and begin to train seriously for the Olympics. You can avoid hunting wild pheasants, an option that concedes the battle before it starts. Finally, you can use the one organ that is supposed to work better in people than it does in either bird dogs or pheasants—the brain. Pheasants rise in front of flushing dogs either because they have made a mental error or because they have exhausted their possibilities on the ground. Unless you enjoy running wind sprints against competition that will always be faster than you, establishing yourself at the end of a limiting terrain feature with the dog working the birds toward you is the way to make optimal use of a flushing retriever's ability. Such natural barriers take many forms in typical western pheasant habitat: creek bends and oxbows, especially in light of the ringneck's enthusiasm for thick river bottom escape cover; high, abrupt banks, as are often found in western coulee country; and isolated fingers of brush that lead from escape cover toward sparse grass or cultivated fields.

The possibilities go on. The essential skill is being able to anticipate what pheasants will do when pressured and where they will eventually flush.

Needless to say, this style of upland hunting is far removed from what takes place behind classical pointing dogs. Teamwork is critical to success in this game, and such teamwork involves hunters and dogs alike. While I enjoy hunting alone, I do appreciate the presence of an experienced hunting partner when I'm working educated ringnecks. This is especially true of the two or three people I hunt with regularly. Working a stretch of cover in such company often becomes a series of back and forth drives in miniature, a style that takes the fullest advantage of the things flushing retrievers do best.

One reason so little has been written on the subject of training flushing retrievers is that there is so little to say, although we shall return to this neglected subject in detail in a later chapter. A dog that is out of control obviously should be on the birds' payroll rather than your own, no matter how lovable your canine friend may be. Above and beyond stop-and-go basics, the difference between a serviceable dog and a great one usually owes more to instinct and experience than to training, a hard admission for those of us who would like to take more credit for the good ones than we deserve. Since I live in an area with long seasons and lots of wild pheasants, my dogs train on the job. Good thing, because there is almost no other way for them to practice effectively.

Whatever the breed, it is important to realize that the qualities that make great retrievers do not necessarily make great flushing dogs. In duck blinds, the hunter controls the pace of the hunt, and style on the part of the dog often boils down to how tightly innate canine energy can be focused on the intentions of the hunter. In upland bird work, on the other hand, it is the dog that often determines the hunt's tempo, and individual qualities of initiative and intelligence become irreplaceable. Such qualities are hard to coach.

Few things in life predictably improve with age. Wines, cheeses, and pheasants hanging in cool, dry places come readily to mind. To this short list I would hasten to add flushing retrievers, who seldom become accomplished until their fifth or sixth season. For several of my own, their best years also happened to be their last before they retired to the rug in front of the fireplace. So be patient, and treat the good ones like the treasures that they are.

It is the last day of a long upland bird season. The leaden sky sits heavily on the shoulders of the prairie and the sun is nothing but a dull, indistinct presence above the distant southern horizon. I am alone except for my dog, Sonny—a state of affairs that seems to capture the mood of the day perfectly.

After two months of hunting, the easy birds are gone and those that remain conduct themselves fluently in the art of survival. They are all holed-up now, in the thickest of the CRP, the most horrendous cattail tangles, and here, in a coulee so choked with thorn apple and buffalo berry that the range cattle can't even get through it. With all due respect for the pointing breeds, this is no place for a dog that looks as if it should be posing for a picture on a calendar. This is knucklehead country.

An earthen dam's bare shoulders rise above the cover a quarter of a mile in front of us. There might still be some open water behind it, but the possibility of jumping a mallard dinner invokes all sorts of lead shot–steel shot legal complications, so I ignore it. Besides, waterfowl season goes on for two more weeks, but the stretch of cover below the dam promises to hold the last pheasants of the year.

The dog knows what to do. He is hunting smart now. His occasional early season reversions to puppyhood have been tempered by weeks worth of cagey ringnecks. He follows quietly to the lip of the coulee, but when I send him down the bank, he hits the cover with absolute abandon.

This is an old, familiar game for both of us. If I were to go down into the brush with him, I would never be able to see enough to shoot. If I paralleled his course on the edge of the cover, the birds would simply flush from the other side, out of range. But we have other things in mind.

With the dog all but lost to the cover, I cut across a bend in the coulee and position myself up on the dam. There are a dozen mallards tucked away behind it in a splash of open water the size of my kitchen table, and I stand at port arms and watch them rise into the winter sky with an ambivalent sense of regret.

Now I can see Sonny cross an opening in the heavy cover a hundred yards away, tail alive, nose to the ground, his attention perfectly focused upon the unseen vector of a running bird known only by its scent. My hands close reflexively on the familiar weight of the double and then the first of the birds reach the dam and the end of the cover. A pair of hens flushes to my left and then a rooster is right in my face, cackling angrily before folding at the shot. There follows a chaotic minute of pheasants, shooting, and dog work as I pick two more cocks from the riot in progress, and then there is nothing to do but enjoy the retrieves, scratch Sonny's ears, turn my back on another bird season, and walk on off into what's left of the year.

Late season ringnecks can be a piece of cake, it seems, as long as you've got yourself the right hunting partner.

I have friends who just don't understand. They cannot imagine why I live in upland bird country without a kennel full of stylish pointers. When I take them bird hunting, they wonder why I always seem to be where the birds are getting up. They question the lung-straining pace of the pursuit and shake their heads at what seems more like chaos than strategy. Wouldn't it be easier, they are always asking, if I got myself a pointing dog and saved those crazy Labs for the ducks?

I won't argue about what might be easier. I will not even point out that these questions are often asked over a dinner of pheasants that would never have arrived at the table had we spent the day hunting with dogs other than my own.

I will argue, however, that the flushing retriever is capable of giving something special where it counts. When you have watched your dog outwit a particularly wily rooster in a way made possible only by years of teamwork in the field, the retrieve and the weight of the bird in your hand and the taste of the pheasant dinner that follows can become their own measures of style.

Sanctuary

Verbal inflation is so common in Alaska that it's important to be precise when describing any structure in the bush. A building with more wood than Visquene in its walls qualifies as a cabin; add a floor and you've got yourself a lodge. Even though the Duck Shack has all this and more, we have always called it a shack because that's what it really is. No marvel of design, it measures barely twelve feet on a side and will accommodate four people comfortably, six with some patience and understanding, and eight in a real pinch. These figures reflect the fact that it is almost always so nasty outside in southcentral Alaska during waterfowl season, that hunters will put up with all sorts of inconvenience in order to be warm and dry.

The Duck Shack's walls are simple plywood painted mud brown. Sloppy technique and years' worth of repairs have inadvertently turned this motif into a camouflage pattern of its own. The shed roof is covered with layers of tar like the annual growth rings on a tree, and the best thing that can be said for it is that it doesn't leak—much. Wooden pilings hold the whole structure up above the saltwater mud flat beneath it. The flats flood on extreme tides about a half-dozen times a year, and we all know that these supports will erode away someday and collapse, at which point we will have to start all over again. Those who build on the tide flats had better get used to the second law of thermodynamics, because entropy is always out there ready to start gnawing away at your accomplishments when you least expect it.

Structurally, the Duck Shack's most elegant feature is the small, open stoop between the steps and the door. When the weather allows, you can sit there in the evening and drink a beer and watch the sun go down behind the looming, snow-covered peaks of the Alaska Range, which makes this one of the most beautiful front porch views anywhere. In season, there are almost always Labrador retrievers lying around on the stairs. Dogs are not allowed inside the Duck Shack—period. This is one of the few house rules. In fact, this may be the only house rule. Anyone who doesn't understand this apparent indifference to our canine friends has never shared a tiny room with a hot stove and four wet retrievers.

The Duck Shack is situated on the remote west side of Cook Inlet. Wracked by immense tides, awash in glacial debris, and hovering above the freezing point even in the middle of the brief northern summer, the Inlet is one of the world's least forgiving bodies of water. It serves as a marvelous physical and mental barrier between the relatively civilized Kenai Peninsula, where there are roads and jobs and mortgages, and the wilderness on the Inlet's west side, where there are no such distractions between man and the important things in life. According to the Coast Guard, after five minutes in the Inlet's waters a healthy sailor can no longer participate in his own rescue. In another ten, he will be dead. Flying across the Inlet on a clear day with beluga whales frolicking below you on the surface, it is easy to forget about those numbers, but they are always there, lying in wait like predators.

Access to the Duck Shack is exclusively by aircraft. It sits beside a pond large enough to accommodate a float plane, and there is also enough solid ground along the edge of the nearest tide gut to allow a Super Cub to land on tundra tires. This is an important detail, since some of us flew floats, while others preferred wheels. When I lived on the Kenai Peninsula, it was only a thirty-minute flight from my house to the Duck Shack, but it felt more like a voyage to another world. The dog would sit in the Cub's backseat and breathe down my neck as we flew, but he was always calm when it came time to land out there, even when he shouldn't have been. Make that flight a time or two with an airplane full of gear and you'll know why Alaska Labs are bred on the small side.

Situated near the entrance to Lake Clark Pass, the Duck Shack was strategically important at all times of the year. Flying home from a caribou or ptarmigan hunt, one often emerged from the pass to find nasty weather hanging over the Inlet like a pall. Home seemed so close and yet so far away, and that's just the kind of temptation that kills pilots. Stopping at the Duck Shack rather than pushing the weather was a wonderful option that we all exercised freely. In this potentially hostile environment, the Duck Shack exuded security. If you made it there, you had made it.

The place was always wonderfully provisioned and appointed, at least by bush standards. No one ever took anything back from the Duck Shack except trash that couldn't be burned, because someday, somehow, someone was going to need it. It contains one of the world's great collections of canned food. Shotgun shells of all gauges line the shelves, for it is one thing to get weathered in at the Duck Shack and another to get weathered in without any ammunition. The library is extensive. This collection does not include many of the great works of western civilization, because one goes there in large measure to get away from western civilization. On the ambitious end of the intellectual scale, one might find, say, the nearly complete works of Louis L'amour. From there, the Duck Shack library descends from the banal to utter trash—Jacqueline Susanne, Harold Robbins, books that can be opened at random to any page without having to worry about losing your place. I have read them all, and at least in that setting I can assure you that the pursuit of literature doesn't get any better. And of course the library provides additional security against the ultimate wilderness crisis—running out of toilet paper.

The Duck Shack contains no end of necessary supplies and luxuries: av gas, oil, tools, dog food, wader repair material, pancake mix, whistles, whetstones, maps and charts, nuts and bolts, tobacco, salt, stove wire, extra clothes and sleeping bags, Coleman stoves and lanterns, duct tape, writing paper, duck calls, decoys, soap, dishes—you name it. If you can run out of it in the bush and have its loss ruin your day (or your week, depending on the weather), it's probably there. Throw in a reliable oil burning stove and a lifetime supply of number two diesel, and you have the closest approximation to the womb since the real thing.

This is rich country from the outdoorsman's standpoint. The streams in the area support strong runs of silvers. August scouting and blind-building trips almost always featured fresh salmon on the dinner menu. Someone usually collected a moose near the Duck Shack each fall, and one year a visitor shot a brown bear right on the Cub strip—but it wasn't much of a brown bear, and it wasn't much of a story. Even so, there were enough of the big bears around to keep you on your toes, especially when things went bump in the night outside the Duck Shack's flimsy walls.

The principal sporting resource of the west Cook Inlet tide flats, how-ever, is waterfowl. Everything is done differently in Alaska, and water-fowling is no exception. As a general rule, any outdoor sport attempted within reasonable distance of Alaska's road system is a waste of time, which is why my friends built the Duck Shack in the first place. Even the birds seemed different there, and we certainly didn't lack for variety. While we were too far inland for the real Aleutian specialties and exotic

Asian strays—smews and pochards and Baikal teal—it was rare for me to spend a day on the flats without having to consult my bird book about something. Snipe were plentiful, and I always carried a pocketfull of No. 9s for those long walks home through the grass. Sandhill cranes were also abundant and their odd, ratchety cries echoed constantly across the flats during duck season. Known colloquially as Eskimo turkeys, they were legal game and welcome table fare, although their wariness and superb vision made them a surprisingly challenging quarry. Tundra swans, on the other hand, were a protected species, although this certainly didn't stop me from appreciating them. Every one of the tide flat's myriad potholes seemed to support a nesting pair, and they decoyed like great white dreams. On still mornings, you could hear them cooing softly in the distance and then they would materialize from the mist, suspended improbably above the blocks as if they were somehow lighter than air.

The ducks themselves were familiar enough for the most part—mallards and pintails and wigeon and teal not unlike puddle ducks anywhere else except for the setting in which we hunted them. It was the setting that made the hunting there so special, with active volcanoes looming behind every shot, tidewater seeping back into the brown bear tracks just ahead of you, and the isolation, the incredible, wild isolation that was always enough to make you feel small beneath the lead gray autumn skies. Some days you would enjoy brisk shooting for a mixed limit over decoys and other days you would have to crawl on your belly for a duck dinner, which means that the duck shooting there had lots in common with duck shooting anywhere else. No, except for the strange, otherworldly atmosphere on the wild side of Cook Inlet and the camaraderie of the Duck Shack itself, the duck hunting on the flats was simply duck hunting, ordinary and wonderful at once.

The goose shooting was another matter.

The place we went for serious goose shooting isn't really called Beluga Island, of course. But our collective obsession with these geese at times approached Ahab's obsession with his own white whale, so it seems as good a pseudonym as any. I make no apologies for this evasion. That's just the way it is with secret places.

Fifty-one weeks a year, more or less, there are no geese on Beluga Island, but it is a major staging ground during the fall migration. Birds don't fly on instruments, and if the weather socks in while the migrating flocks are there, they will have to stay until it lifts. This means that three thousand honkers may be packed into a limited area with nothing to do but cruise around in circles and make noise and watch the sky for a break in the clouds. It also explains the essential dilemma of the hunt—if the weather is nice enough to make a flight to the island a reasonable proposition, it probably isn't worth going. And vice versa.

There is a gravel ocean beach on the southeast side of the island that offers a low-tide landing site. Inland from the beach lies the island's one true tide flat, and that is the place where the geese will be if there are any there at all. You can pull an airplane up above the breakers and tie it down in the drift logs where it should be secure against all but the highest tides. It sounds so simple now, described on a typewriter from the security of my desk some three thousand miles south of the Duck Shack. Alaska, let us remember, has ways of fooling you when you least expect it.

The definitive Beluga Island goose hunt, the one that is still talked about in solemn tones around the stove at the Duck Shack whenever its survivors gather there, took place one stormy October day when the geese were in. There was a high tide late that afternoon, and the idea was to pull the Super Cubs up above the tide line, shoot a limit of geese, and take off from the beach once the tide had started to fall in order to make the trip back to the Duck Shack before dark. The trouble is that sometimes even veteran hunters get excited, and the cacophony of geese circling just behind the logs on the beach made everyone, including those who should have known better, forget about the effect the strong southeast wind was going to have on the incoming high tide.

Covering ground always takes time on the flats, where mud sucks hungrily at your boots and tide guts force you in directions you don't really want to go. Even though the distances were small and the shooting fast, it took several hours to complete the hunt, by which time—you guessed it— the airplanes were bobbing around in the surf like bathtub toys.

One was a total and immediate loss. The second was salvaged from the waves at no small risk of hypothermia. By this time it was dark and there was nothing to do but huddle among the flotsam with the dogs and spend a miserable night trying to keep a fire going. The following morning, the sky was cold and clear. The one salvaged airplane limped into the air to begin an evacuation back to the Duck Shack. The geese were leaving too, and one can imagine a certain vindictiveness in their noisy cries as they departed.

Even then the great Beluga Island goose hunt wasn't over. Its memory kept returning to haunt its participants like a mummy's curse. Some five years later, part of the salvaged Cub's tail fell off in flight, probably as a result of corrosion damage sustained during its saltwater immersion on Beluga Island. Using throttle, trim tabs, and considerable skill, my hunting partner was able to get back on the ground intact, at which point the last of the Beluga Island Cubs was stripped down for parts on the spot.

The geese still stage out there in the cold Pacific each fall, and every year I think of them when they do, even though I no longer live in Alaska. It is one of the world's great goose shoots when the conditions are just so, and my partners still fly off to Beluga Island from the Duck Shack each season in hope of finding the right conjunction of birds and weather to reproduce one of those manic hunts. But none of us will ever listen to the cries of migrating geese without being reminded of the night the cruel sea reached out for us on that distant beach, and nearly caught us all.

Of course, ours is not the only duck shack on Cook Inlet. Closer to Anchorage, small communities of similar structures sprout on the flats and on the opening day of duck season there is more air traffic over Knik Arm than Anchorage International. Inevitably, the thought of all those people having such a good time began to bother somebody, and around the time I left Alaska there was a movement to get rid of all the duck shacks. They were said to be an eyesore, to be ecologically disruptive— you know the drill. Of course, they are all so remote that it is unlikely any of the offended parties had ever actually seen them, and as long as their owners were responsible about trash and cleaning up after themselves (we were meticulous, I can assure you), their environmental impact was negligible. Behind all those lofty concerns, of course, was the grim hand of the anti-hunters. For a while, those of us for whom the duck shacks were a way of life had some anxious moments. The state, which owns title to all tidal lands in Alaska, finally came up with a compromise worthy of Solomon: a moratorium on new construction on the flats and grandfathered ninety-nine-year leases on existing structures. Everyone was happy except the diehard animal rightists, who seem constitutionally incapable of being happy about anything worthwhile. At any rate, the Duck Shack still stands.

As well it should. The tide flats of Cook Inlet are a fantastic outdoor resource that cannot be enjoyed except by the hardy. The environment is so harsh that it is not feasible to be there without some sort of protection from the elements. If there were no duck shacks, no one would even know what was out there, much less care, and in these times of trial for the preservation of wild places, we all know what that means. And that is why the environmental wing of the anti-duck-shack movement had it all wrong, despite what were no doubt the best of intentions.

Weathered, listing, and cramped, the Duck Shack is no palace, but I miss it. When the oil stove was kicking and the wind was driving the rain against the walls outside, it did everything that architecture can do for human beings. Neither the company inside nor the wilderness outside could have been any better. It allowed us to remove ourselves, at least temporarily, from the demands of modern life across the Inlet and provided a necessary sanctuary from all sorts of worry. The waterfowl themselves at times seemed almost incidental.

It was a sanctuary for all of us, hunters and retrievers alike. Waterfowl deserve sanctuaries, and we do, too. I am proud to have enjoyed this one and the corner of the wilderness it allowed me to know.

Early Birds

There is no reason to get up in the dark except that I want to, and since I want to very badly, I am sitting bolt upright in bed seconds before the alarm sounds, a truly mysterious exercise in ESP that anyone can acquire after enough anticipation on enough opening days.

After yelling downstairs to Nick and putting the coffee water on the stove, I step outside on the porch to stretch and smell the new day and enjoy one of the great physiologic conveniences of country living. A dull glow has started to appear in the eastern sky already. Little more than the absence of darkness now, it still serves notice that the first shooting light of the year waits just beyond the horizon. We may even be a few minutes late this morning, but since we are not hunting waterfowl or turkeys or big game, it really doesn't matter. And since I have two professions and a long list of outdoor pursuits that force me to pay attention to clocks and sunrise tables and deadlines, the ability to take my time this morning is a pleasure to be savored.

I used to have one of those automatic coffee makers, the ones that look like computers and flash green digital warnings all night long and finally wake you up with the explosive sound of coffee beans grinding. The idea was that this device was supposed to spare you the bother of making coffee, but I discovered that I actually enjoyed the bother of making coffee, so when mine broke I never even tried to fix it. We're back to basics around our house now, boiling water over the stove and dripping it by hand through a conical filter into a glass carafe. From there, my coffee goes into an insulated Circle K mug with a lid on top so that it won't spill, even if I'm driving down a rough road or being jumped on by an enthusiastic retriever. It occurs to me that if Circle K did everything as well as they made coffee mugs, Wall Street might have treated them more kindly.

As I pour the hot water through the filter, the dog climbs up the stairs and begins snuffling around the kitchen with more interest than usual. Soon he is panting and wagging his tail, and I realize that somehow he has figured out that we're going hunting. That's a bit spooky, since I'm not even dressed yet and it's difficult to imagine what a Labrador retriever might sense about this morning that is different from any other morning when I have to get up early because of responsibilities at the hospital or some deadline I've ignored for too long. Perhaps it is the game vest sitting over on the dining room table or the smell of gun oil lingering in the air that gives the show away. On the other hand, perhaps I just look happier than I usually do when I get up in the dark. Intuitive critters like Labs seem to be sensitive to that kind of thing.

There has been no sign yet of Nick, my fourteen-year old son. I remember the security of sleeping in a few extra minutes on opening days long gone. Having a father around to worry about the details is like having a snooze button on the alarm clock—both can be relied upon to wake you again before any real damage is done. The time has come, however, and I tell the dog to go downstairs and get Nick out of bed. That command in not in the vocabulary of most field trial champions, but it is certainly useful around our house. Moments later, I hear the sound of a large dog jumping up on a bed followed by wet, face-licking noises and sleepy cries of adolescent protest, and then Nick is in the kitchen beside me.

It is a half-hour's drive to the ranch we plan to hunt this morning, and the sun is creeping over the edge of the plains by the time we arrive. There are plenty of disadvantages to having your eldest child reach adolescence, but there are compensations as well, one of which is that Nick is at last big enough to open ranch gates. This is a three-gate patch of sharptail cover, but this morning I get to sit inside the cab behind the steering wheel and drink coffee while Nick puts his shoulder into the fence posts and wrestles with the wire. In another year he'll be driving and in a few more he'll be gone, and I am suddenly aware that we ought to be doing as much of this kind of thing as we possibly can together before that happens.

The two-track ends above a shallow coulee studded with silver buffalo berry bushes. The ground cover here is all natural grass, and in the low, rich, morning light the complexity of its color is visually stunning. The conventional wisdom holds that the West's natural beauty is concentrated high in the mountains, and for selfish reasons I'm glad most people seem to accept this as fact. On prairie mornings like this, however, it's an easy argument to refute. While the dog is off sniffing, I ease into my shooting vest and watch Nick remove his 20-gauge Lefever from its case. I've hunted with kids Nick's age who had to be watched in the field, but Nick seems to have been born cautious. It is gratifying to note the care with which he loads and handles the gun. This has not been an easy summer in many ways, and the feeling that I may actually have done something right in my life is certainly welcome, if not downright overdue.

Finally we set off toward the brush. When the prairie has enjoyed a wet summer, as it has this year, the grass can be thick enough to clutch at your feet when you walk, and when it is, birds are likely to be scattered, since they do not have to depend on the buffalo berry bushes for cover. Thick ground cover is one of the defining features of early season sharp-tail hunting, especially when you can find grass like this that has not been overgrazed by cattle. You may have to cover a bit more country in order to find birds, but when you do, they are likely to be cooperative.

For years, one casualty of my passionate love affair with the longbow (and there have been several) has been the opening day of bird season. Traditionally, Montana's archery and upland bird seasons (exclusive of pheasants) both opened on the first Saturday in September, and despite my enthusiasm for dogs and shotguns, I just couldn't tear myself away from those bugling elk long enough to go bird hunting. Now bird season opens on the first of September no matter what day of the week that falls on, which means getting to go through all that manic opening day behavior twice in a matter of days. This morning, enjoying the opening of bird season without distractions from big game feels as welcome as sitting down to dinner with an old friend.

The grass is heavy with dew, and after walking through it for a half-mile, my boots have soaked through and my socks are starting to squish with every step. Suddenly, the dog seems to focus on the early morning thermal currents with new intensity. His interest might seem subtle to the untrained eye, but after all these years on the prairie I have no trouble reading the presence of game in his behavior. Off to my right, Nick is wandering toward the nearest brush without paying any attention to the dog, but before I can shout at him, the first birds flush.

Later in the season, the sharptails will be wild, appearing, for the most part, as distant targets to challenge the reach of my tightly choked Parker, but they are still young and cooperative now. These have held in the dense grass and flushed close enough to let us appreciate the checkered markings on their breasts and the warm, rootbeer-colored hues along their flanks. Above all, close sharptail flushes like this are auditory affairs.

The wingbeat is rapid but powerful, with more bass to it than Huns or pheasants will ever provide, and the alarm cry that invariably accompanies the flush is as rich and rolling as a Scotsman's burr. In a month or two, the cover will be thinned by grazing and weather, and the birds will never let us get close enough to enjoy all this, but now they are there at point-blank range, suspended in the morning air just for us.

The first pair splits the imaginary spatial plane between Nick and me and I hold my fire, not for reasons of safety but because I would much rather see Nick drop one of the birds than shoot one myself. I have taken my share of sharptails over the years and, as much as I enjoy all these goings-on, I don't need to shoot much in order to have a good time out here anymore. Nick probably doesn't either, at least if I have raised him right, but there is still a childish flush of pleasure when a bird drops cleanly. And so I keep my shotgun's muzzle pointed up toward the sky and watch as he mounts his double and swings on the bird nearest him.

Nick is at that awkward half-man, half-boy stage of development during which it is hard to get an accurate reading on a kid's physical skills. He is fast enough to do well on his school's track team, and I stopped inviting him to jog with me nearly a year ago out of a petulant sense of embarrassment at the ease with which he outran me. He is an accomplished competitive skier, and watching him on the slopes fills me with wonder. His hand-eye coordination has always been suspect, however, and when I first put a shotgun in his hands I thought he might be in for a difficult time. In fact, he proved to be a natural, a genetic ability I'm sure he inherited from his grandfather, although there are occasionally days when I have to wonder if this is one of those hereditary traits capable of skipping generations.

As for this morning, well, sure enough. The bird crumples at the Lefever's report and the fact that he forgets about the second half of the potential double doesn't even register at first. There will always be time for doubles. I watch to be sure that he does not commit the excited novice's error of running toward a downed bird with one barrel loaded and the safety still off, but he stands calmly, marking the fall and collecting himself.

"Reload!" I urge. "There's going to be more!" He breaks the double and the rest of the covey flushes as if on cue. One confused bird flies straight at my head and I respond with the old grouse hunter's trick of pivoting and taking him straight away, converting an impossible angle into what would be a routine low house station seven on the skeet range. I hear the sound of the Lefever's action snapping closed, followed by two quick shots from Nick's 20-gauge. Then the covey's last trailer is crossing at the edge of my own range and I swing and fire, sending the bird tumbling far down into the coulee.

I do not train my dogs to be steady to wing and shot because I don't want them to be. When birds are down, I prefer that they be busy doing their job rather than looking stylish. Sonny is already halfway back with the first bird in his mouth as Nick and I reload, check our safeties, and regroup.

"What did you get out of that second rise?" I wonder aloud as the dog delivers the first sharptail to my hand.

"I dropped one over there," Nick says, pointing toward a cluster of wild roses. "I missed him with the first barrel," he admits sheepishly.

"That's still good shooting," I assure him, remembering how such a simple bit of praise from Nick's grandfather used to feel when I was that age.

The dog has brought in my own first bird by now and I give him a line toward the wild rose cluster. In contrast to pheasants, sharptails pose few problems once they are down. They seldom run and they lack the ringneck's tenacity when evading dogs, but even so, in thick cover such as this, recovery would be a chore without the services of an experienced retriever. Sonny makes everything look easy today as he emerges from the brambles with the bird in his mouth, and we walk to the edge of the coulee to search out my long fall.

"I marked the rest of the covey down over there," Nick says, pointing with his forefinger as the dog bounds away down the sidehill.

"Tell you what," I observe as I watch the dog and try to remember my landmarks in the coulee's jumbled bottom. "I think we've taken enough out of that bunch for today."

"Then we should keep going toward the bushes," Nick suggests hopefully.

"This was supposed to be a quick hunt," I remind him. "You've got school. I've got work."

The dog is making game far below us, and finally he pounces on the last bird. Certain that he has done well, he holds his head at a jaunty angle as he scrambles back up the hill with the bird displayed like some sort of trophy. Five shots, four birds, no losses; the morning's line score feels nearly perfect. Overhead, the sun has started to assert itself and my guess is that it's only a matter of time until the thermometer creeps up into the 80s. One thing years of experience in the field teach you is when it's time to quit.

"Let's just hunt our way back to the truck," I suggest. "Thick as the grass is out here this year, there could be more birds anywhere. Besides, we've got a grouse dinner and you've got algebra."

This isn't quite the verdict Nick wanted me to reach, but it is too nice a morning to argue and he knows it. The dog is still eager as we swing back toward the rig parked in the distance, but the grass yields nothing except an occasional meadowlark. Across the coulee, a herd of antelope crosses the skyline. The buck bringing up the rear looks like a good one and I stop to study his horns as he pauses, silhouetted against the morning sky. Even without binoculars, I can tell that he has everything—length, mass, and prong—and I file this bit of intelligence away for archery season.

Back at the truck, we unload the shotguns and slide them into their cases. The dog has started to pant in the mounting heat and I pour water from a five-gallon can into a dish so that he can drink. Nick is staring wistfully toward the distant line of buffalo berry that we never even reached. He wants to keep hunting, but he is old enough to begin learning about the perpetual conflict between sport and obligation. There is nothing comforting to say about this subject, so I say nothing, and we kennel the dog and climb into the truck to begin the three-gate trip back to the county road and home.

And there you have it, a simple tale involving less than two hours of hunting and a handful of shells. There is nothing epic about this opening day, no furious shooting or sagging game vests or heroic performances by the dog, and yet I cannot get over the idea that our morning's work embodies something close to the heart of the matter. Our quarry is a simple, under-appreciated native. Hunting them appeals to my well-developed sense of tradition, as does the enactment of opening day rituals with my own son just as my father did with me thirty-odd years ago. I can number the opening days that remain before Nick goes off to college on the fingers of one hand, and we will not have to shoot boxes of shells or limits of birds in order to make each one of them count.

We stop at the first of the gates and Nick climbs out as the rest of the world waits for us on the other side.

Here Today

I found the snipe field purely by accident. It was the last week of an unusually clement August and one could almost ignore the fact that the brief Alaskan summer was about to end. The signs were there to read—the decay of dying salmon in the lower reaches of the rivers, the sudden edge in the morning air's bite—but we all chose to ignore them in a collective suspension of disbelief. My goals involved fly rods and silver salmon that day as I flew across Cook Inlet and landed on the edge of the tide flats. Hunting was certainly not the first thing on my mind, but then it's never far behind no matter what the circumstances.

I had to work my way up a mile or so of river to find the fish, but they were worth the effort—mint-bright silvers in the twelve-pound range that struck savagely and ran and jumped and made my fly reel sing. I kept one for dinner and released all the rest, and when the sun arced behind the peaks of the Alaska Range, I set off toward the airplane for the short hop over to the Duck Shack, where I planned to spend the night.

The hike back took me across an open expanse of grass flats. The ground underfoot was damp and spongy enough to make walking a bit of a chore, but I was still flush with enthusiasm from the fishing and scarcely noticed the extra effort. There had been bear tracks all up and down the sand along the river, and I was being careful as I walked, since some of the grass was thick enough to hide a snoozing sow with cubs—not a group of bears you want to blunder into armed with a fly rod. That prospect made me just edgy enough to turn inside-out when the first snipe flushed underfoot.

Wilson's snipe bear a close resemblance to dowitchers and a passing similarity to a number of other shorebirds, but from the sportsman's perspective, there is one overriding difference—snipe take to the air like something you would like to shoot with a shotgun. This one erupted from the grass in a marvelous explosion of wings and by the time I recovered from my own startled reflexes, I was tracking its flight across the tide flat with the muzzle of an imaginary double.

That bird was just the first of many. In fact, I have never seen a concentration of snipe anything like the birds that flushed out of the grass that afternoon. Alaska can be hungry country for the upland gunner, with little besides hard-earned ptarmigan and occasional fool hens to vary the regular diet of waterfowl. While we all took snipe from time to time walking to and from duck blinds, this was the first time I had ever seen anything to make Alaska's generous snipe limit sound like anything but an abstraction. With the migratory bird season due to open in a matter of days, all those snipe looked like an invitation to a sure thing.

I spent the opening morning of duck season at our cabin enjoying the usual combination of good company, unruly dogs, and slow gunning that prevails before the weather turns cold. After lunch, I dug out the box of trap loads I had brought along for just this purpose and announced that I was going snipe hunting. Everyone looked at me as if I had gone crazy. As noted earlier, opening days at the Duck Shack are occasionally interrupted by the urge to take moose, cranes, silver salmon, and even brown bears, but an organized expedition in search of snipe was without precedent. Offering no explanation other than a sly smile, I tossed the dog into the back of the airplane and took off for the snipe field, confident of an impending triumph. The idea of all those envious looks from my hunting partners and a skilletful of braised snipe to compliment our dinner was almost more than I could stand.

The snipe field, of course, turned out to be utterly barren. It was not just that some of the birds had disappeared, or even most of them. They were all gone, to Canada or Mexico or somewhere, and I know because the dog and I covered every inch of the grass flat with relentless determination. It takes a lot to make an experienced Lab look discouraged, but mine was obviously having second thoughts about the afternoon, when a misguided teal roared by overhead and I dropped it just to smooth things over.

Back at the cabin, there were lots of jocular comments about the missing *hors d'oeuvres*, snipe hunting in general, and my judgment, all of which I took in stride as I remembered the birds that had been there scarcely two days earlier.

Let them laugh, I told myself. I knew what I had seen. Honest.

Ducks, geese, doves, and snipe share one trait in addition to the pleasures they provide in the field and on the table. They all have sense enough to go south for the winter and to come back home again in the spring. If we were not constrained by jobs, families, and financial obligations, I imagine that most of us would do pretty much the same thing, which may say more about the relative intelligence of humans to water-fowl than any of us should readily admit.

In the meanwhile, those who define their own relationship with these species in terms of shotguns and retrievers and hot ovens have to come to terms with the fact that the objects of all that desire are not above stand-ing us up on a regular basis. As in the pursuit of anadromous fish, it is quite possible to get up in the dark and endure all kinds of fumbling in woolens and waders only to find that the quarry has forgotten the engage-ment entirely, or moved on to bigger and better things. Philosophers in the crowd will no doubt claim that this builds character.

Well, I am not a philosopher. I do not expect the birds I pursue to fly straight or flush on cue or live in convenient places, but I do ask that they be in the general vicinity when I set out to find them. Pheasants may run and grouse may hide and chukars may require you to break a few more contour lines, but migratory species are quite capable of abandoning the area completely, by moving on to the next swamp, or to the next conti-nent. It hardly seems fair.

Consider, for example, the case of the mourning dove. When I was a kid growing up in Washington state, we would scout the doves trading in and out of the fields for days before the season began. By the time we were ready to go hunting, we usually knew just where we wanted to be when the season opened. We always kept those appointments, but the doves were another matter. One hint of autumn in the air would be enough to send them south, often, it seemed, without taking time to pack. This exodus took place with remarkable consistency on the first day of dove season, plus or minus twenty-four hours. During the good years, we enjoyed furious shooting on the opening weekend and the rest of the time we sat and looked at the empty blue skies that the doves had just aban-doned for the somewhat less blue skies of California. I have nothing against the residents of that state, no matter what you might think. I just wish they had let me shoot more of their doves when I was a kid.

When I moved to Montana twenty-odd years ago, there was no dove season, for reasons that were never clear to me. Come September, doves would be everywhere while we were hunting sharptails and Huns, but there wasn't anything we could do about it except watch them. I noted with interest that these Montana doves seemed to thrive in chilly weather that would have sent the birds I knew as a boy fleeing south. Finally the state of Montana came to its senses and realized that there was no reason to raise doves just so we could send them south to be shot by hunters in

Texas. The week before Montana's first dove season, I located vast flocks of birds feeding in a hailed-out wheat field. Anticipating fast shooting and my first dove dinner in years, I arrived on opening day to find (surprise!) that the birds had all flown south, a performance they have repeated every year since then.

I don't know why regulatory agencies endure all the turmoil they go through in order to set the opening date of mourning dove season. They should just declare in perpetuity that the season will open one day after the doves leave whatever state I am living in and be done with it.

Ducks are certainly not beyond pulling these great disappearing acts either, and in my corner of the Central Flyway, no species is more likely to do so than the blue-winged teal.

I've always been partial to blue-wings. They are beautiful, challenging on the wing, and a delight on the table. When I lived in the northeastern corner of Montana during the pre-drought era, blue-wings usually dominated our early season bag. As noted in an earlier chapter, blue-wings were ten-point ducks then in the Central Flyway's point system of limits, which meant that you could shoot a bunch of them, a generous allotment fully justified by their abundance.

Our enthusiasm was partly driven by the knowledge that they wouldn't be there for long. In fact, the departure of the blue-wings was usually the first natural phenomenon to announce that the end of summer was at hand. There were years when we never got to hunt them at all. When things went well, we would set up the decoys on one of a number of little sloughs just outside town every morning during the first week of duck season. We would shoot limits of blue-wings before work and eat teal for breakfast, lunch, and dinner. Then one day they would all be gone, leaving us to hunt upland birds and await the arrival of migrating mallards. In a good year, we would get a solid week of teal hunting before their disappearance, but even then the feel of every shot was tempered by the knowledge that the target might be the last of its kind for the season.

Because of what is at stake when we hunt them, geese carry the ability to frustrate by unscheduled absence to extremes. There are no skies as empty as those over a goose pit when the geese have gone, especially when you have hacked the pit out of frozen ground and crawled into it in the dark and lain there supine for hours in the cold like a corpse in a tomb. Of course you will be reluctant to rise and start picking up the decoys because of all the times the geese have chosen that precise moment to arrive in the past. So you will lie there and stare at the sky all morning until either your bladder or the last vestiges of your judgment cannot stand it any longer. When you finally leave the field, you will feel like the victim of a vast, elaborate practical joke—and in a sense you will be.

One fall afternoon in Alaska, a hunting partner called to tell me of a tremendous congregation of geese on a nearby tide flat. I loaded the airplane and flew out to the spot during the last hour of daylight. The ground looked black with geese from the air. By the time I landed on the beach and set up a rudimentary camp above the tideline, it was too late to shoot. The dog and I fell asleep to a chorus of goose talk, but when we awoke the next morning, the marsh was silent. I felt like a bride abandoned at the altar as I stared out across all that emptiness. I wound up jump shooting a limit of mallards from the grass which mollified the Lab somewhat, but the ducks felt like little more than a consolation prize as I walked back toward the airplane with the noise of all those geese echoing through my memory like a hallucination.

Of course there is another side to the sometimes maddening disappearance of migratory birds from our lives, and the ability to keep such matters in perspective when nothing seems to be going right out there may be the most important principle of all.

One October evening some years ago, Dick LeBlond, my hunting partner, and I picked up our decoys and began the long slog out of our favorite marsh after several hours of waterfowling that could only be described as relaxing. The weather was calm and still, which never helps. The blue-wings were long gone and we had been forced to settle for a smattering of odd ten-point puddle ducks. We were both working young retrievers, however, and the unhurried pace of the shooting had been just right for them. The dogs had done well and there had been plenty to look at in the marsh, so no one was complaining in spite of the slow shooting, especially since we were hunting instead of working, which always serves as a personal definition of time well spent.

We were halfway back to the truck when the first flight of mallards sailed by overhead. A few minutes of shooting light still remained and we had plenty of room in our limits, but by the time I got myself untangled from the decoy bag, the birds were beyond us. Then a slow rumble began to descend from the darkening air like a jet liner on final approach to an airport, and before we knew what was happening, the air was literally full of ducks.

Plump northern mallards numbering well into the thousands, they had already decided where they were going to spend the night and our presence was not about to stop them. The air quivered from the sound of their wings as they settled into the marsh grass all around us. Dick and I both started to raise our guns and then in a rare moment of common sense, we lowered them again without firing a shot. We were right on the trailing edge of legal shooting light, but the decision to hold our fire went beyond such concerns. It just did not seem possible that shooting ducks was going to add much to our fascination with the spectacle in progress.

Ducks in such vast flocks enjoy herd instincts of their own, and once the collective decision to land has been made, the usual tenets of caution no longer seem to apply. The air fanned by the mallards' wings washed against our faces as they flared to land, and the dogs leapt wildly in undisciplined attempts to catch them. They were not successful, but they came close. The arrival of the flight went on and on, until it did not seem possible that there could be any more ducks in the sky, and then the great noise stopped at last and there was nothing left but the soft, warm chuckle of contented mallards all around us in the night.

As I closed my eyes and let the feel of the birds' presence press in around me, I thought of all the times ducks and geese had stood me up and left me shivering alone beneath impassive skies. Then it all was clear to me at last—the teeming mass of thousands that had taken our breath away was someone else's heartache. Somewhere to the north, disconsolate gunners were staring into empty skies of their own and wondering where their ducks had gone and how they could have left so abruptly.

There was a symmetry contained in this realization that helped put countless missing doves and ducks and snipe and geese into proper perspective. Nature turns out to be a stickler when it comes to balancing accounts. What leaves here can only arrive somewhere else. The idea is to spend enough time in the field so that everything will come out even in the end, which it will, as long as we are patient enough to let it.

Dick and I called the dogs in and settled them down as best we could, which was no small task, since we were still in need of some settling down ourselves after being engulfed by all those ducks. The decoy bag felt lighter somehow as we followed the light in the western sky back toward the truck. As the hike settled into an easy rhythm of its own, I listened to the mallard noises recede behind us and imagined the ducks as a river, as opposed to a lake—fluid, ever-changing, defined by their inseparable capacities to delight and disappoint.

Here today, gone tomorrow. The rest is up to us.

Ruffs Out West

The coulee behind my house hardly looks like good ruffed grouse habitat. Its rolling terrain does not contain a single abandoned apple orchard or stand of beech. There are no alder thickets to engulf the gunner, the dogs, or the quarry. The sighing ponderosa pines that line the hillsides remain defiantly green long after more classical grouse coverts have wrapped themselves in the golden mantle of fall. And when I walk through those trees, as I do several times a week nearly every week of the year, the terrain evokes no memories of dog work or brilliant shots or even brilliant misses. This final shortcoming alone makes suspect the coulee's credentials as ruffed grouse cover.

And yet the birds are there, in numbers that would arouse the attention, if not the outright excitement, of most eastern wingshooters. I hear them drumming in the spring whenever I sit quietly against the base of one of those pines and yelp and and await the company of a Merriam's gobbler. After the first autumn snow, I see their tracks winding aimlessly beneath the thorn apples as I scout for whitetail scrapes. In between, nothing marks their presence but the birds themselves, but I have learned to look for them peering back at me from the recesses of the brush, and I see them often enough to make any dedicated ruffed grouse hunter take notice.

But I don't take notice, at least not the way a predator would take notice. I suppose that means I am not a dedicated ruffed grouse hunter anymore.

It certainly hasn't always been that way. The first bird I ever killed on the wing was a ruffed grouse. I was ten years old at the time. I was supposed to be twelve, but after years of watching me handle guns, my father made an executive decision and allowed me to hunt two years before the state of New York thought I was ready. My father is ordinarily not one to trifle with the rules, but he felt that hunting with his kids was important enough to justify this exception, a transgression for which this particular kid will always remain grateful.

I still remember that first ruff. Our old shorthair pointed and my father flushed the bird and let it rocket away in my direction. The grouse passed at right angles, and when it hurtled through a gap in the trees, I swung and slapped the trigger going away and it tumbled in a cloud of feathers and amazement. That was certainly one of the seminal experiences of my childhood, my own personal version of the shot heard round the world. From that moment on, I hunted ruffed grouse nearly every waking moment of every day of bird season until my family moved west and left our familiar grouse cover behind forever. Out here, distracted by a wealth of more abundant game, the once pre-eminent ruff became little more than a memory and an occasional benign distraction.

And it is in the spirit of that memory that I slip down into the coulee today wearing a game vest and carrying an over-and-under. The shotgun is not the same one that I hunted with as a kid (that still rests in my father's gun cabinet a thousand miles away), but it is a virtually identical Browning, worn smooth by two decades of constant use in my own hands. Today, it feels just the same as the one that I used to carry, as it balances in the crook of my arm, and that is important somehow. There are few measures of continuity as certain as the feel of good guns.

The greatest distinction between today's exercise and the grouse hunting I did as a kid comes from the dog kennel. As much as I love my Labs, I wish that I had a shorthair with me now. In the first place, the pursuit of ruffed grouse without the services of a pointing dog feels incomplete somehow. There is nothing wrong with the idea, but it isn't quite what I came for. Grouse hunting is just so intrinsically canine, and the dog part of it has to do with the sudden silence of a belled collar and the intimacy of a pointer frozen rigid as a statue in the autumn woods.

Furthermore, it is hard for me to remember anything about my early ruffed grouse hunting career that did not involve German shorthaired pointers at a very fundamental level, and above all else, today's hunt is firmly grounded in nostalgia. My westernized kennel has evolved to keep pace with my current interests. While there is still plenty to choose from, those choices are all Labrador retrievers and lion hounds, and it's a bit hard to imagine any of the lot focused on a ruffed grouse down in the brush.

Today, Sonny is the dog that really needs to go hunting. I release him from the kennel, and after his obligatory sniffing trip around the house, we cross the fence behind the barn and head downhill through the pines toward the grouse cover, such as it is. My frame of mind is ideal for this adventure. I took an antelope buck with the longbow yesterday and that accomplishment has tempered my need to bowhunt, at least for a day or two. This morning, the old black dog and I kicked a limit of sharptails out of the brush at the edge of the prairie east of town, so the keenest edges of my own predatory instincts have already been satisfied. The day is warm and still overhead and the cool depths of the sheltered coulee beckon. It seems a perfect time to explore the shadowed corners of my property, and of my memory as well.

The grouse will be concentrated in the strips of thorn apple near the bottom of the coulee. The route downhill takes me underneath a neglected whitetail stand and I file its obvious need of repair away in my mental notebook of unfinished chores. Then we cross a swath of disturbed mast left behind by a foraging flock of turkeys. The sign is fresh and fall turkey season is open. I stop and listen and study the open areas on the hillside across the coulee, but the woods have swallowed the whole flock somehow and the turkeys will have to wait for another day. All that is fine with me. This afternoon, I am a grouse hunter once more.

While there is plenty going on in the coulee to occupy my attention, Sonny is getting twitchy. I left him behind this morning so that I could work with the older dog, and he is not happy about the affront. Now he is straining at my side, and to tell the truth, I am not quite sure what to do about it. The role of a flushing retriever in the pursuit of ruffed grouse is not intuitive, and I have no historical precedents to guide me. Somehow, I imagine that we will work it out when the time comes. In the meantime, I release him from his position at heel and let him bound away through the pine trees just to get him out of my hair. He is happy just to be hunting, and so am I.

It is a fifteen-minute walk down through the open pines to the thorn apple and there is something to look at every step of the way. A scattering of white, curlicue bird droppings identifies the tree where the turkeys have been roosting. A line of fresh scrapes marks the way of a whitetail buck. It occurs to me that I have never found an arrowhead on my own property. Of course, there were no whitetails or turkeys here a century ago, and the area's native inhabitants enjoyed richer hunting grounds on the open prairie to the north and east. Perhaps our own culture has not been as bad company to wildlife as we sometimes imagine.

At the bottom of the hill, I whistle the dog back to my side and study the cover. The nature walk is over, for the time being at least. The problem now is how to turn a stroll along this paltry tangle of scrub brush into a grouse hunt. The solution promises to require both faith and lightness of heart.

With the dog's role still undefined, I keep him at my side and start down the line of brush. I know what eastern ruffed grouse would do in this situation. They would carefully wait until there was as much cover between us as possible and then they would erupt from the other side, using every available scrap of thorn apple to screen their retreat. With only one gun along today, that tactic would almost certainly be successful. But I know something else as well—these are not eastern ruffed grouse.

The first hundred yards of cover produces one giant puffball, one four-point whitetail drop, and a lot of heavy breathing on the part of Sonny. Both the puffball and the shed antler wind up inside my game vest, insuring my afternoon some objective measure of success whether the grouse make an appearance or not. As for the dog, I keep him at heel because I cannot imagine how he will help me running blindly through the cover on his own. Then I hear it—an agitated cooing something like a turkey's putt rendered through an alto sax. Eastern grouse hunters might spend seasons in the woods without ever hearing this sound, but it is familiar to me as the alarm cry of a nervous ruff.

The noise is coming from deep within the thorn apple tangle. I stand at port arms and wait for an explosion of wings but nothing happens. My dignity abandoned, I crouch and then drop to my knees and there it is, a dark shape strutting nervously away through the brush.

The urge to turn around and walk away from all this silliness is beginning to acquire a life of its own, but I have come too far down memory lane for that. I want to shoot this grouse and I want to shoot it right. After a half dozen steps backwards to open up some shooting lanes, I send in the dog.

Delighted to discover both freedom and a sense of purpose at the same time, the Lab charges into the brush like an angry rhino. His nose locks onto the bird's scent line at once, and then the noise of wings against brush fills the air. I brace myself for the explosion and the wonder of the hurtling target but as soon as the bird clears the thorn apple, the flight aborts. I watch crestfallen as the grouse settles onto a low-hanging limb in the nearest pine. The bird stares at me. I stare at the bird. The dog tears on through the thorn apple, desperate in his attempts to conjure a shot and a retrieve from this comic situation.

Good grief.

And there you have it, the essential dilemma of the western ruffed grouse hunter. On the other end of the continent, the ruff is wily and demanding, a virtual signature defini- tion of sport on the wing. Out here, biologically identical representatives of the species almost always find ways to dis- appoint you, no matter how accommodating your intentions. They think and fly like rocks. They are more likely to frustrate than to challenge. They are, in short, fool hens.

That is why I can count on my fingers the number of Montana ruffed grouse that I have taken with firearms. I refuse to shoot them on the ground (or from trees) with anything but a bow. This principle flies in the face of local custom, which holds it permissible (if not downright admirable) to behead limits of sitting ruffs with rifles in order to provide table fare in hunting camps. While I don't have a problem with this on the part of others, I've never been able to bring myself to do it, no matter how badly I might long for a ruffed grouse or two on the table. The memory of the birds with which I began my wingshooting career just won't let me.

For those were different birds entirely. Back then, there was a season limit of forty ruffs in New York. The reasons for this limit were never clear to any of us, as it seemed as impossible to attain as it was to enforce. Then one year my father actually did it, an accomplishment owed in equal measure to our exceptionally capable shorthair and Dad's own ability to hit things on the wing. No one in town could remember anyone shooting a season limit of grouse before, and this achievement became the occasion for much celebration on the part of everyone but my father himself, who suddenly found himself with two whole weeks of bird season on his hands and nothing left to do.

Those partridge were the kind of gamebirds that inspire true devotion. Their counterparts out west are not, and since the state of Montana offers generous seasons and limits on Huns and sharptails and ringnecks (gamebirds that inspire devotion once again), it is easy for hunters like me to ignore the western version of the ruff, except as an occasional aside with bow and arrow or elk camp *hors d'oeuvres.*

And remembering how great it used to be only makes such ignorance easier.

But not today. Perhaps it was the sentinel suggestion of autumn in the air this morning, or the blush of yellow in the deciduous trees scattered among the pines. Perhaps it was the old shorthair in the back of someone's pickup at the grocery store yesterday, staring into my eyes as if he expected me to recognize him, or even to take him hunting. We will never know, but the fact remains that today is a day that will not feel complete without a ruffed grouse in it, to explode and command my attention and make the double swing.

So what am I to do about the bird sitting overhead? If I were carrying the bow, I could drill it and still feel good about the afternoon. If one of the kids were with me, I could hand over the gun, throw a pine cone at the grouse to make it flush, and thoroughly enjoy whatever happened next, no matter what the outcome. If I had a young Lab along, I could shoot the bird myself and justify the assassination as a training mission for the dog. But here I am, alone with Sonny and a 12-gauge shotgun and a fool hen sitting in a tree. There is only one civilized thing to do, which is to shake my head and walk away, and that is the option that I finally exercise.

The dog follows reluctantly. He knows that there is still a bird back there somewhere, and he is not disappointed by the impossible standards of another time and place. A mouthful of warm ruffed grouse would suit him just fine, no matter what romantic ideals we compromised in its taking. It occurs to me that life would be less perplexing if we could all live it like Labrador retrievers. Sometimes they just seem to know so much better than we do.

For us, matters are more complicated. Nature does not disappoint, I tell myself as the dog and I start back up the hill toward home. It is we who disappoint ourselves. And there I am, wrapped up in all that philosophy, when the dog noses his way into the cover and another grouse erupts from the last reaches of the thorn apple and presents itself on the wing in so much less time than it takes to tell. The bird is suddenly framed by a window in the brush, where my own reflexes manage to get the shot column right on schedule, without the least bit of urging. The grouse's death is inevitable by then, and when it comes, it is nothing more than the abrupt absence of noise and motion on the other side of the bushes. Then the dog is presenting the bird and I realize that against all odds, I have done it. I have gone home again.

There is new vigor in my legs during the steep climb out of the coulee toward the house. I feel ready for autumn now, ready for whitetails and turkeys and the rest of my life. Sonny is unhappy with the track we are taking. He wants to forge on through the cover, to find more game, to do it all again. The grouse was just another bird to him, a reason to keep on going rather than a reason to turn back toward home.

This time, I am the one who knows better.

Zen in the Art of
Partridge Hunting

The first covey flushed wild as Huns so often do. It was a lazy prairie afternoon, with just enough breeze to maintain its own sense of direction and not even a hint of the first hard frost of autumn, even though a cold snap was coming in less than a week. Hunting season was still young enough to allow several hours of shooting light after work, but there wasn't enough time to set up an elk hunt and the weather was too hot to sit a whitetail stand, so I took the dog to a ranch north of town and set off across the rolling terrain with an agenda every bit as relaxed as the afternoon itself.

We were working the edges of some sharptail cover to no avail when the Huns rose from the shoulder of the hill above us. Because of their almost random distribution in cover that scarcely qualifies as cover in the first place, a Hun covey's rise is almost always a startling event, like a backfire on a crowded urban street or an unexpected summons to the boss's office. One minute there was nothing but the quiet sounds of the prairie and the dog, and then a cacophony of squeaks filled the air, as if every stubborn metal gate on the ranch had been prevailed upon to open at once. A blur of wings followed and there were the birds, a baker's dozen of them rising and turning as one, all packed into a sphere of airspace so small that it looked as if a single load of shot should have been able to drop them all. Of course, those of us who have been there before know better, and I have been there before. Believe me.

They were out at the very edge of shotgun range, far enough away so that they looked like a swarm of motion rather than a collection of individual birds. The gun rose halfway to my shoulder as if by its own accord. I thought about shooting and the dog thought about breaking in pursuit, but we both had just a bit too much experience under our belts to let a flock of Huns make fools of us that easily. Discipline prevailed, and we stood and watched the birds wheel their way around the side of the hill and set their wings for the long, free ride down the coulee. When they finally settled into a patch of grass a half-mile away, I had their location marked and the dog danced around in anticipation as if he had them marked, too. One of us was lying, but it was too nice a day to start an argument.

It took us fifteen or twenty minutes to hike down the draw and work our way up the side of the coulee toward the spot where I had last seen the birds. Suddenly, the variegate patterns of grass all started to look the same, and I realized that we were lost. I was walking along with my gun over my shoulder and the dog at heel when the birds flushed wild for the second time. Once again, they rose in a sudden eruption of noise and wings, and there was nothing to do but watch them sail back across the coulee toward the same contour line where all of this had started.

This time they settled in just downhill from an isolated juniper that served as an ideal landmark. Like Sysiphus' stone, I rolled back downhill and then waited for my legs to pull me up the other side again. Could it be that the Huns were playing with us? Of course not. That was too anthropomorphic an idea, too conceived a notion. They were just being Huns; we were the ones who had made the choice to pursue them.

And I did know one important thing about uncooperative coveys of Huns—after two or three wild rises, they will usually hold and flush one or two at a time, offering as fast a flurry of wingshooting as the prairie is ever likely to provide. The trick, of course, is staying with them until they do. They will predictably put as much contour behind them as they can each time they flush, and if they get around a corner in the terrain so that you cannot mark them down, you may have to start all over again. This is clearly a game for young hearts and optimistic spirits.

As we closed upon the solitary juniper, I kept the dog at heel. The birds themselves would determine our need for his fine nose soon enough. Silence prevailed as we eased forward into the ankle-deep grass where I had marked the end of the covey's flight. Huns seldom run, and the dog's attitude indicated bird scent in the air all around us. Although it didn't seem possible that the sparse ground cover could hide anything larger than an insect, we both knew that the birds had to be there, virtually underfoot.

I clucked my tongue at the dog, releasing him from my side. He lunged forward with his nose to the ground and a single exploded from the grass, a sudden blur of gray and chestnut in the Indian summer sun.

The bird cut sharply downhill behind me and I pivoted in the opposite direction to drop him going away. I stopped the dog with my whistle and hesitated before reloading. Another single justified my caution when it rose to the left and crumpled at the second barrel's report.

All of us—the Huns, the dog, and I—had been operating at the very margin of our self-discipline, and now, finally, the tension simply became too much. As I snapped the double open and fumbled frantically through my vest pocket for more shells, the dog crept forward, seduced by all that bird scent in spite of himself. A double rose from the grass and departed the hill in opposite directions. I closed the gun hastily and missed the closer of the two with one barrel at marginal range. Forgetting the principle I had so neatly demonstrated a moment before, I opened the gun to reload only to watch two more birds rise right in front of me as I did so. Fumbling with the whistle and a pocketful of shells at the same time required more hands than I posses. Shells fell to the ground. The dog reluctantly sat back on his haunches. Birds rose. I swore.

Finally, the gun was loaded and ready. As the dog and I started up the hill together past the little juniper, all the chaos and confusion of the moment seemed to recede behind us. My breathing settled into an easy rhythm of its own and it felt as if the prairie itself was flowing right on through me. When the final pair of birds rose, the gun found its own way to my shoulder, following a path made familiar by the dozens of seasons it has spent with me in the field. The two shots were the doing of my hands and my eyes and the shotgun, and the birds confirmed the simplicity of it all by folding on the wing and tumbling together toward the earth with precise and nearly indescribable grace.

Now it was the dog's turn. He collected all four birds easily, in the reverse order of their fall. His enthusiasm seemed larger than he was somehow, and I sensed that he would keep on hunting there until he died, if only I would let him. But the final double suggested a certain perfection upon which we could not improve. I called the dog back to my side once more, and this time when I opened the gun to eject the two spent shells, I did not reload.

The Huns had given us everything we needed to make the afternoon complete. There was nothing left to do but start back toward the truck, as free and easy as the breeze itself.

Most prairie gamebird species do not offer much technical challenge on the wing. The terrain is open, in contrast to classical eastern grouse cover, and sage hens, sharptails, and pheasants are all basically large, ponderous birds that offer few surprises in flight. Those of us who have been at this for a while should be forgiven if we occasionally long for something to test the limits of our skill with the shotgun, something that has nothing to do with beautiful western scenery, loyal bird dogs, and all the rest of those warm, fuzzy considerations writers like me are always trying to plaster all over our hunting seasons.

No, I am now addressing the notion that wingshooting is in itself a worthwhile art, at least if we think of art in the oriental sense, as a discipline whose mastery can lead to realization. There are qualifications to this idea, of course—no game-farm birds, no unsportsman-like conduct, no preoccupation with bag and body count á la Lord Ripon. But once you have made these few small concessions to bio-political correctness and the abstract concept of honor, there is just no reason why swinging a well-balanced double at a fleet gamebird should not qualify as an art form, at least when the swinging is done in the right manner.

Let us call the practitioners of this art pure shooters, to borrow a term from basketball parlance. Above all else, pure shooters value game that consistently provides challenge on the wing. Eastern ruffed grouse and bobwhite qualify. So do chukar, blue-wings over decoys, and mourning doves trading in and out of grain fields. Despite the variety and abundance of upland birds here on the prairie, however, there is really only one to excite the pure shooters in the crowd, and that is the Hun.

The Hun, or gray partridge as it is properly known, arrived here in Montana from its Old World home in roundabout fashion. The bird was first introduced to the Canadian prairie provinces after the First World War, whereupon it migrated spontaneously to the south, entered our country without official permission, and found our combination of stubble fields and windswept hillsides irresistible. No one has ever asked that they be deported, least of all those of us who define our autumns with dog and gun.

In contrast to some other imports, Huns look like they belong here on the plains. They fill their own niche in the short grass that is too sparse for other species to call home, and they have a greater affinity for grain stubble than any other prairie gamebird. For aesthetic reasons, stubble has never been my favorite cover to hunt, but the promise of Huns can make even hundreds of acres of the stuff seem less monotonous than usual. It's hard to imagine what this country would be like without Huns around to fill in all those blank spots in the prairie.

Unfortunately, we seem to be finding out. Something has happened to our Huns. When I first came into this country, it was difficult to do anything outdoors from September until December without enjoying an opportunity to shoot them, usually in limit quantities. We regularly took Huns incidentally while hunting other species as diverse as geese and antelope. Their populations started to decline during the drought years of the early 1980s, and by the time I returned to Montana from Alaska they were all but gone.

The fact of their disappearance is perhaps less disturbing than the mysterious reasons for it or the apparent lack of concern it has aroused. No one seems to know what happened to the Huns and no one seems to care, except for the odd pure shooter hidden away out here on the lonely prairie. In contrast to pheasants and big game, Huns are not a glamour (read, profitable) species, and so the official line is, "They'll come back."

I hope the official line is right.

D ecember. The light arrives low and flat from the southern sky. Conveying none of its expected warmth, the sun disappoints. Another bird season is winding down all around us, but the dog and I have no intention of going gently into the night. We plan to hunt to the end even if everyone else has given up and we can enjoy no company other than our own.

Today we are ignoring the pheasant cover, and not just because of its inherent nastiness. We have been hunting pheasants for six weeks and I am frankly burned out on them, even if the dog is not. I am hunting with Sonny today, a pheasant dog above all else, and I can sense his longing for the heavy cover where his own particular relentless style will best serve us both. Sorry, buddy. That's why I'm wearing a whistle around my neck and you're wearing a collar around yours. Today, we are hunting Huns.

Even as a shameless enthusiast of flushing retrievers, I am the first to admit that their role in the pursuit of Hungarian partridge is less than obvious. In fact, the Hun is the one prairie species that sometimes makes me long for a pointer. But I will also go on record as saying that if you can't hunt it with a Lab, it probably isn't worth hunting, and I am a man of strong conviction, even when those convictions are susceptible to charges of bullshit.

So here we are: the dog, the Parker, and me. I will employ Sonny in two ways today, the first of which he is demonstrating at this very moment. Conceding the first flush to the birds, I've let the dog range far out in the stubble field beside me while I plod along its edge. His purpose there is simply to flush birds I would otherwise never see. For the moment, he is nothing but a nose astride four strong legs, as brainless as a heat-seeking missile looking for an exhaust pipe to ascend. Right now, that is all I ask of him.

A skiff of snow coats the landscape, and while it is scarcely thick enough to hold tracks, there has obviously been plenty of traffic to and from the field and all its leftovers, so free for the taking. Mule deer, pheasants, and raccoons declare themselves one after another in the powder, and then suddenly turkey tracks appear. There are not supposed to be turkeys here. I look up, gauge the distance to the nearest roosting cover, and file this information away in the mental junk box of outdoor data that has swelled over the years to contain an embarrassing percentage of everything I have ever learned.

But today we are hunting Huns, as a ruckus from the field suddenly reminds me. The dog has done his job. A tight covey of a dozen birds erupts from the golden stubble well out of shotgun range. As I track their flight against the snow, they set their wings, string out into a line, and eventually disappear into the thick cover along the nearest creek bottom. Because of the distance, I mark them down a little less precisely than I would like. But there is drifted snow and dense grass where they have landed, and I have the feeling that they will hold without making us chase them all about the country.

The dog returns to my side at the sound of the whistle and we set off toward the distant bend in the creek. He feints back and forth constantly at heel, as if straining against an imaginary leash. The constraints of his training hold true, however, and he is still right where he is supposed to be when we reach the wild roses where I think the birds have landed. Now it is time to exercise the second function of the flushing retriever in the pursuit of gray partridge.

First, I must perform the mental exercise of settling myself in, letting the muscles of the neck and shoulders relax so that the gun can swing without the threat of conscious over-correction. The Huns, I know, will try to get me to do too much, and shooting them honestly and successfully involves, above all else, giving in to a certain inner sense of freedom. Content with the way the gun feels in my hands at last, I cluck the dog forward and wait for the first explosion of wings.

It turns out that I was off by sixty yards when I marked the birds, but with a nose like Sonny's, it all comes down to a matter of time. They can fly, but they can't hide, not from a dog who wants to retrieve a few of them as badly as this one does. As we work our way into the hollow of the creek bend, half the covey rises in front of a high clay bank and two of them go down just like that. One of them looks less than absolutely

dead, so I line the dog out and send him at once, for it will not do to end the season with an unrecovered bird.

That doesn't happen often when you do your upland bird hunting with a Lab, and it doesn't happen today. Sonny even bumps another single from the roses as he returns with the cripple in his mouth, but I just stand and watch the bird fly away, for all sorts of reasons. Lori and I are hav-

ing dinner alone tonight, and two Huns are all we need. There is no reason to have another odd bird or two cluttering up the freezer. And finally,
it just will not do to end the season with a miss either.

We are done, Sonny and I, at least until the end-of-the-year mallards
arrive. The dog still senses the smell of birds ahead of us and he turns
away reluctantly when I call him, although he finally yields to my judgment in the matter. If I have learned anything about this over the years, it
is that it is important to know when to shoot and equally important to
know when to stop shooting.

A breeze is freshening in the northwest. The sun feels cold and futile
off in the bottom of the sky. It is time to turn my collar up and began the
long walk from the field toward the fires of home.

The Versatile Retriever

R ay and I began the morning sitting next to a handful of decoys tucked into a backwater on the river. Most of the water that wasn't moving too fast to hold ducks had frozen, but the mouth of the slough was deep enough so that the ice couldn't quite get a foothold there. We knew that the ducks would come and they did, and then the shooting was done and it was time to let the dogs work.

There had been over two hundreds mallards in the flock. Both of us had doubled, which was no great accomplishment considering the number of greenheads compressed into the airspace above the mouth of the slough. Two of the birds had fallen across the river on dry land, but the other two were bobbing away on the river's main current. We sent the dogs downstream after the birds that we were in greatest danger of losing. There is always an element of terror involved when brave dogs plunge into moving water that is choked with ice, but they were both old hands and there were no mishaps. After they delivered the first two birds, the trip across the river for the second pair seemed purely routine.

As the dogs were shaking the water from their coats, a small set of a half-dozen ducks appeared above the tops of the cottonwoods. We each picked a drake from the flock to complete our limits and then the dogs were back in the freezing water once again. Ray's bird had fallen dead right in the middle of the decoys, but mine was heading downriver on the current with a broken wing and Sky in furious pursuit. Five minutes later, he was back at my side with the bird in his mouth.

We picked up the decoys, stuffed the birds in our game vests, and headed back toward the truck. Our route took us along a frozen, reed-choked slough. There were fresh pheasant tracks in the snow, and we each took one side of the cover and let the dogs work between us. It was a still, clear morning, and the noise the dogs made as they plunged through the dry reeds sounded as if it were being played through an amplifier. Finally a bird flushed, but it was a hen and there was nothing to do but watch as she passed by overhead.

Fifty yards farther down the line, a short spur of brush crawled up my side of the cover and headed toward the adjoining stubble field. I could hear one of the dogs working his way through it as I approached, and then a rooster's angry cackle rose from somewhere in the heart of the reeds. By the time he cleared the top of the brush, he was all noise and brilliance in the cold morning light, as only cock pheasants can be. Sky had put him right in my face, and the shot itself was kid stuff.

I heard Ray shoot twice from the other side of the slough and then he was yelling at his dog, which of course is the only tone of voice in which those who handle Chessies can communicate with their charges. By the time I rounded the finger of cover, Ray's dog had completed his first retrieve and was working on the second. He flushed another rooster in the process. The bird had the misfortune to fly over my head, and I dropped him right out of the morning sun. By the time the dogs were done, we each had a pair of ringnecks to go with our mallards—not a bad way to end a duck hunt.

When we arrived back at the truck at last, there were ten birds in our game vests, not one of which would have been there without the efforts of two versatile retrievers.

The world of wingshooting is a broad one, especially here in the West where a weekend of hunting may well put an ambitious gun in front of a half-dozen varieties of game in settings that range from duck blinds to alpine meadows. For those of us who cannot distinguish the hunt from the dog, this embarrassment of riches poses a real problem. One approach is to have a kennel full of specialists, and to choose among several breeds whenever you venture into the field. The other is to find a generalist, a dog that will do everything.

In the best of all possible worlds, we would have the time and resources to manage the first option. Wide-ranging pointers for Huns, tightly controlled Brittanys for pheasants, hard-charging Chessies for cold water...the possibilities go on. One hesitates to imagine all the game that could be harvested. One also hesitates to imagine the time required to train all those breeds, not to mention the dog food bill.

In fact, the appeal of getting lots of hunting out of one dog goes far beyond dollars, cents, and time. Those who hunt with specialists, for example, might well have walked right on by the pheasant hunt described at the beginning of this chapter. There is a lot to be said for having the right dog with you at all times in the field, and the easiest way to make that happen is to insure that the dog you have can hunt anything that comes along.

One approach to the search for a versatile gun dog is to coax some water work out of a pointing breed. There is nothing wrong with the idea, which was responsible for much of the German shorthair's original popularity in this country. One of the greatest dogs I have ever known was the family shorthair that I learned to shoot over in upstate New York when I was a kid. However, his greatness came in the grouse cover. His water work was not much more than adequate when evaluated objectively, which it will never be easy for any of us to do. Of course, there wasn't that much to ask of him in that capacity, since most of our waterfowling consisted of jump shooting woodies on small water. Given our needs at the time, it would be hard to imagine a dog that met them better.

Twenty years ago, I decided to explore the other option—the versatile retriever—and I have never regretted the choice. Waterfowling was an especially large part of my life in those pre-drought, pre-steel-shot days, and I just couldn't imagine beginning the fall with a dog that was going to cost me unrecovered ducks. In the process of training Labs for water, I also taught myself a lot about using them for upland game, which is fortunate, since there is almost nothing about this subject to be found in print. It is now my firm conviction that the versatile retriever is the most effective pheasant hunting device ever invented, especially in the vast, rugged cover we hunt out west. We have also used these dogs to hunt just about everything else, and while I will not pretend that a Chesapeake Bay retriever can work a covey of Huns as stylishly as a setter, they do get the job done. We have enjoyed enough grouse and partridge dinners over the years to prove it.

The choice of breeds for versatile retriever work is a highly subjective matter. While my own opinions are a matter of record by now, I would not presume to tell all Chessie owners that their charges are anvil-heads, even though this is obviously true.

All kidding aside, if I have learned anything about this issue over the years, it is that most of the conventional wisdom is more conventional than wise. Chessies are capable of real surprises on upland game: I've shot too many roosters over Ray's dogs to pretend otherwise. And although my Dad once had a golden that hunted hard enough to dispel almost all my swamp-collie biases, this breed does not enjoy the obvious superiority on upland game that some of its advocates suggest. Recognizing the subjectivity of all this, I would end the discussion with three suggestions:

1) Don't start with a Chessie unless you have had some prior training experience and are willing to commit a substantial amount of time to the dog;

2) Don't start with a golden if the job description involves a lot of hardcore water work; and

3) Do yourself a favor and start with a Lab in the first place.

With my own prejudices a matter of record, Labs will illustrate most of what follows, although these principles apply to the other retrieving breeds as well. I would also note that I happen to use male pronouns in reference to dogs throughout the following discussion simply because most of my own best dogs happen to have been males. This is certainly not meant to suggest that female retrievers (or anything else) can't get the job done in the field.

Beginning with a puppy rather than an older dog has a number of advantages. As accommodating as these dogs are, bonding never develops as strongly as it does when you raise the dog from puppyhood yourself. The strength of those bonds is responsible for a large measure of the versatile retriever's appeal, and it is a shame to sacrifice those ties for the sake of expediency. Furthermore, it is worth remembering that no one ever sells a good started dog voluntarily, at least not for prices most of us can afford. If you are serious about this, you too will someday have to reach into a wriggling litter of pups and make one of the most important guesses of your life.

A substantial amount of mystique will surround that choice. Classical dog writing emphasizes the careful study of pedigrees, but the object of this scrutiny has never been clear to me. If papers bearing the names of lots of champions guaranteed good hunting dogs, obtaining one would be a nearly mechanical affair and you would already have skipped over the material in this chapter in favor of more hunting stories.

Obviously, I take a somewhat casual approach to pedigrees. (If this attitude bothers you, wait until you hear what I have to say about guns in the next chapter.) It is my experience that of every four pups chosen for training, one will be excellent, one will be useful, and the other two would better be directed toward pursuits that do not involve hunting. Selectivity can improve those rough odds somewhat, but not much. Rather than procrastinate endlessly like Hamlet, it is usually more productive to pick a pup from some reasonable litter and launch yourself into the training process without further ado.

A review of retriever training's fundamental elements is beyond the scope of this discussion. There is already plenty of good information in print concerning basic obedience work and training retrievers to retrieve. For those who have had little or no training experience, those are the right places to start. Basic retriever training techniques form the foundation for training the versatile retriever, and the discussion that follows assumes some familiarity with these methods.

Training retrievers to hunt upland game is another matter. There are important differences between teaching a Lab to fetch ducks and teaching the same dog to hunt pheasants. The retrieve itself is a logical task that lends itself well to human control. The hunter can actually do most of the thinking, while the dog becomes an instrument of the hunter's intention, more useful for the ability to mark, swim, and cover ground than for the ability to hunt on his own. Commands are largely given from close range, where they are easy for the dog to interpret and for the hunter to enforce. Retrieves pose few problems that cannot in theory be solved by a computer, and those are the easiest sort of solutions to teach.

The flushing retriever used for upland game has a far more complex job description. These dogs must function independently to a far greater degree than their duck blind counterparts. Since the hunter is often unaware of just what the birds are up to, there are often no commands to be given, and yet the dog must be aware at all times that the hunt is a team sport in which it does no good at all to flush birds in the wrong places. The solutions to the problems posed by running pheasants are not always logical, and they certainly cannot be neatly diagrammed and reproduced in the backyard. Finally, both the dog and the hunter must learn to be flexible, for no amount of training can prepare either of you for all the different situations that will eventually arise in the field. Training flushing retrievers means training hunters as well.

It is important to bear in mind that training a flushing retriever involves a fundamental shift in the dog's sensory orientation to the world around him. Classical retriever training emphasizes what the dog can see, but you are going to have to emphasize what the dog can smell. This is a difficult task for a number of reasons. Olfactory acuity varies tremendously from dog to dog as all experienced trainers know. Unfortunately, it is difficult to asses a given dog's nose until you are well into the training process. Furthermore, we are severely handicapped by the woeful inadequacy of the human nose. When a dog misinterprets visual cues, we can at least identify the problem and address it. When a dog misinterprets olfactory cues, we are often none the wiser. All this makes training the flushing retriever a difficult proposition for trainer and dog alike, which may be one reason the subject has received so little formal attention.

The process begins with the basics of obedience. Flushing Labs don't need to know how to shake hands or roll over, but they had better know how to sit, come, stay, and heel, and you have no business trying to advance their education until they do. In the process, I like to introduce them to training dummies and begin their education in traditional retriever fashion, as if there were no plans for upland gunning in their future whatsoever. Beginning with basic retriever training allows the dog to get to know me and to develop an enthusiasm for the training process under simple, straightforward circumstances. There will be plenty of time for confusion later.

A dog that is going to hunt with his nose needs to be introduced to live birds, and in the case of the flushing retriever, the sooner the better. Even so, the basic rule-of-thumb for introducing dogs in training to live birds is that if they are not yet capable of following appropriate commands without live birds present, they are not ready to try training with them. Only when you are comfortable with the dog's grasp of basic commands and performance with the dummy is it time to introduce your friend to birds. This process will always go better if the introduction takes place in the controlled environment of the training area rather than in the field during the course of a hunt.

Start by working the dog on shackled pigeons just as you would in traditional retriever training. At this point, the bird is little other than a warm-blooded (and wonderfully odiferous) training dummy. Don't try anything fancy until the initial hysteria has passed and the dog is comfortable retrieving live birds. All dogs—all good ones, anyway—will be overeager in the beginning. The idea is to avoid putting the dog in a position in which he is likely to do something with the bird that requires negative reinforcement (like trying to eat it), at least until he is familiar enough with birdwork to know that it's his behavior, rather than the bird itself, that is the cause of the punishment. Failure to follow this principle can dampen a dog's enthusiasm for birds beyond repair.

Once warm feathers are a matter of routine, it's time to start letting the dog learn to track. Begin by having the dog watch a shackled pigeon wander away in front of him on open ground. The dog will be tracking visually, but there will be plenty of time to work on his nose later. The idea at first is simply to enforce the notion that the object of the retrieve—the highest form of reward to a retriever—is a moving target rather than a static one.

As soon as the dog is comfortable tracking moving birds across open ground, and his manners are good enough so that you no longer have to scold him for romping or hard-mouthing, it is time to let him start tracking with his nose. Begin in grass just deep enough to hide the bird. With the dog sitting at heel, release the bird and let it wander off until it is out of sight before sending the dog on the retrieve. Increase the time and distance that the dog must hunt with his nose in a progressive fashion. Of course, shackled birds don't always cover as much ground on foot as we would like, especially in thick cover. Using pheasants instead of pigeons helps if they are available. Domestic ducks are another alternative. You can also increase the amount of time the dog must rely on his nose by walking farther and farther away from the site of the bird's release with the dog at heel before sending him on the retrieve.

When he can do this satisfactorily, you can start releasing the bird prior to the dog's arrival in the training area. This is the time to make the philosophical transition from *"fetch"* to *"hunt."* It is more than a matter of vocabulary. I stop giving the dog precise directions at this point, because that implies that I know just where the bird is, when, under actual hunting conditions, I won't. All you are supposed to do is introduce the dog to the area to be hunted; finding the bird is now his responsibility. Release the dog from heel and let him find the scent line on his own. While the retrieve itself will serve as his reward, it never hurts to lavish a little praise on your charge for a job well done.

After he has played this game a few times, repeat the process with a check cord on the dog and teach him to stop on command while trailing the bird. I prefer a single explosive whistle blast to communicate this command because it will carry well in the field. The whole point of this exercise is simply to teach the dog under controlled circumstances that he must obey commands as usual even when he is hot on the scent of a bird (and believe me, he won't want to at first). Remember that you can't really teach a dog to track, but you can teach him to be under control while he's tracking.

You can also teach him to hunt where you want him to hunt. Just as his superior nose is essential to the partnership between you, so is your (allegedly) superior brain. Now is the time to teach the dog to cast in the direction you want him to hunt. Even though I make every effort not to over-control my dogs in the field, there are still frequent situations in which you need to be able to direct your dog toward likely looking patches of cover or places where you just *know* a bird is hiding.

The groundwork should be laid by introducing the dog to hand signals in the backyard in usual retriever training fashion. There are important differences, however, between casting and handling. The latter, as traditionally taught to retrievers, is a tightly controlled process in which the dog is stopped and then sent in a specific direction with a specific goal—a fallen bird—in mind. Casting, on the other hand, simply encourages the dog to hunt in a general area at the discretion of the handler. No specific reward is implied. In the field, the best a dog can hope for when asked to hunt in a given area is the chance to find a bird. When I command a dog to take a hand signal, in contrast, I am in effect promising him a retrieve, at least if he does everything right. I think it is important that the dog appreciate this distinction.

Once a dog has some familiarity with hand signals, he can be taught to cast by working him on planted birds. In contrast to tracking exercises, this will go best if the bird doesn't move after it is planted—pigeons work well for this purpose. When you arrive at the field, release the dog from heel and let him start hunting. Approach the bird from downwind, but at some distance lateral to the bird's scent line. As you draw closer, call the dog's name to attract his attention and then give him a "soft" hand signal in the direction of the bird. Ideally, he will start in that direction, scent the bird, and wind up making the retrieve. Once this response has been enforced, you can begin to increase all the involved distances. The object of this exercise is to teach the dog to pay attention to you as you move through the field together, and to enforce the notion that hunting where you ask him to hunt increases his chances of finding a bird.

Training dogs always involves adding progressively more difficult tasks to an established foundation of canine knowledge. It's easy to apply this principle to the situations outlined above. Increase the length of time between the bird's release and the dog's arrival in the field to get him used to tracking colder scents. Start him farther and farther away from the point of release, to teach him that it pays to keep hunting even when the hunting isn't very good at first. Work him under different scenting conditions and in different kinds of ground cover. The more variables you can expose him to under controlled conditions, the easier the transition to hunting conditions will be.

As you prepare your dog for upland bird work, don't forget that the final goal is a truly versatile retriever. Good performance while tracking and flushing birds is no excuse for sloppy retrieving. Keep bringing the dog back to basic retriever work to reinforce the traditional principles of marking and handling. I like to end each training session with one crisp, formal retrieve as a means of reminding the dog of his roots.

If you plan to use your dog on wild ringnecks, remember that he will be most useful to you in the nastiest cover around, as suggested in earlier chapters of this book. Some dogs seem to come with built-in enthusiasm for thorns and heavy cover, while others need a bit of encouragement. It will help to find out which category your dog falls into before you take him pheasant hunting. If he seems to think that wild roses and buffalo berry aren't really part of his job description, there is work to be done. Basically, you can either make the cover more appealing than the open ground that the dog prefers, or you can make the open ground more unappealing than the cover.

The first option is usually easier for all concerned. Once the dog has progressed to the point of tracking live birds through grass enthusiastically, this is easy enough to arrange. Begin by planting a shackled bird just inside a typically uninviting patch of brush. Lead the dog immediately to the cover, line him out from your side, and command him to retrieve. The idea is for him to discover the bird as soon as he makes contact with the cover. Retriever instincts should take over from there. Once he is hitting the brush with enthusiasm on command, you can start to lengthen both the time and the distance between the command and the reward, which is, as always, the retrieve. Introducing a dog to heavy cover in a controlled fashion is certainly more productive than letting him out of the truck for his first pheasant hunt and expecting him to figure this out for himself in the midst of all the inevitable distractions.

This is an opportune time to comment on electronic training devices. Shock collars (as they will always be known despite the efforts of their manufacturers to soften their image with euphemistic names) certainly sound useful when it comes to controlling headstrong dogs at great distances, and they can be. To inexperienced trainers, however, I would offer one important caveat: Learn to use electronic training devices correctly or do not use them at all. While there will always be a great temptation to haul out the shock collar when a young dog starts misbehaving in the presence of live birds, yielding to that temptation will be a disaster unless the electronic device is used as part of a comprehensive training program. To use these potentially effective devices in a haphazard fashion is to abuse them, not to mention the dog.

The fact is that there is only so much you can do to train a flushing retriever in the back yard. Some trainers advocate introducing flushing dogs to wild birds during the off-season, essentially allowing them to continue the sort of training exercises outlined earlier on birds in the field over the course of the summer. There are several problems with this approach. In the first place, it is illegal in some states, including the one I live in. Turning bird dogs loose on familial coveys can be hard on wildlife whether the dog catches any birds or not. And purely from a training perspective, the whole point of working with shackled birds is that the dog has a built-in reward—the retrieve—at the end of each successful trail. The best a dog can do on wild birds before the season is to flush the bird he is tracking, and that's not really what either one of you is after.

At some point, you are going to have to take your canine friend hunting. No matter what kind of gun dog you are training, his first introduction to the real world of wing and shot may be the most critical juncture in the dog's development as a useful companion in the field. In the case of the flushing retriever, this initiation is especially important because there is so much to learn that can be taught in no other way. In fact, I freely admit that I spend a lot more time teaching my dogs under hunting conditions than I do in the artificial training situations outlined earlier, but that is because I am fortunate enough to live in a place where I can hunt wild birds four months a year.

Opinions vary about when young dogs should begin to hunt. Rather than adhering to rigid formulas, I prefer to keep an open mind and make an individual decision based on each dog's personality and performance. Remember that a dog's first season should be fun, above all else. If the dog requires constant correction in the field he isn't going to have fun, and neither are you. It is best to hold such dogs back a bit, keeping in mind that a dog can mature considerably between one season and the next. Certainly, the usual mistake is to ask too much too soon. That is a good argument for keeping new dogs coming along at regular intervals, so that you never need to hunt a young dog before he is ready. On the other hand, I've had dogs that were an absolute pleasure in the field before their first birthday. It seems criminal to deny dogs like that an opportunity to hunt just because some authority thinks they are too young to do so.

How you introduce a dog to the field is usually more important than when. There should be as few distractions as possible during the dog's first actual hunting experiences. That often means having no kids, visitors, or inexperienced hunters along, and it absolutely means no other dogs. If those circumstances are difficult to come by, leave the young dog in the kennel until the very end of the hunt and then let him out to explore a little bit of cover while everyone else waits back at the truck. Turning a

novice dog out into a field full of shouting, whistling, and shooting distractions is a prescription for sensory overload for the dog and discipli-
nary melt-down for the handler.

Given the opportunity, I would like to exercise some choice of species
for a dog's first hunt. Ringnecks are graduate school material. So are
chukars. Sharptails enjoy an historical popularity for training young
dogs, which is why professional trainers used to cart their charges off to
the Canadian prairies for their finishing work. Since sharptail season
opens a full six weeks before pheasant season in my country, most of my
dogs have enjoyed the good fortune of starting their careers with these
cooperative birds. Sage hens would be my second choice, Huns a distant
third. Many hunters who lack the opportunity for such variety will have
to start with pheasants no matter what, in which case they should realize
that they are offering their young dogs a trial by fire.

Above all else, your own attitude remains central to the dog's development during the critical first season. The dog should be the focus of the
hunting experience. If you have been working hard all week and feel that
you absolutely need to shoot a limit of pheasants to maintain your own
mental health, your long-term agenda will be better served by leaving the
trainee at home and hunting with a veteran. Try to avoid putting yourself
in the position of requiring too much of the dog. Hunting often forces
dogs to deal with situations for which no amount of backyard training can
prepare them. In the absence of experience, the young dog will have to
learn some things by trial and error. At first, even the errors should be
fun.

All honeymoons must end, and in the case of the versatile retriever,
this transition takes place during the dog's second hunting season. It is no
longer enough to have fun—the dog must now start to do what you want
him to do in the field. By this time, the dog should have enough positive
experience behind him to know that he isn't being punished for going
hunting. One of the Labrador retriever's most endearing personality traits
is the ability to absorb discipline constructively. Faced with the need for
discipline in the field, goldens may go to pieces and Chessies are likely to
respond with maddening indifference, while Labs typically act mortified
just long enough to let you know that you have made your point, and then
it's back to business. The second season in the field is the time to take
fullest advantage of this characteristic.

As noted earlier, flushing retrievers develop slowly and usually don't
come into peak form until their fifth or sixth season. This is precisely
because there is so much for them to learn that cannot be learned by any

means other than hunting. These are the years in which partnerships between hunter and hunting dog truly thrive.

And it is that element of partnership that is the final measure of the versatile retriever's appeal. Field trial quality pointers and water dogs can be handled with cool precision by emotionally distant professional trainers, but the flushing retriever will never hunt for anyone the way he will hunt for the hunter who raised and trained him. Thoughtful hunters will realize after a few seasons that, in addition to training the retriever, they have been training themselves, for hunting with every good dog of the lot is really an art in its own right. My style in the field changes in subtle ways to accommodate the individual style of each of my dogs. That is not something I would do casually, but the best of my dogs certainly deserve it.

It's official now. According to the latest information from the American Kennel Club, the Labrador retriever is the most popular dog in America.

There is good news and bad news contained in that simple fact. On the one hand, all those Labs are obviously not headed for field trials, which means that the versatile retriever may be on the verge of getting some respect. On the other hand, it is also likely that the future of the breed will be determined to an increasing extent by people who do not hunt at all, which is at least of theoretical concern. Let us remember that the poodle was once a working breed. Will the collective soul of "our" Labrador retriever be stolen away by forces indifferent to the hunt? Possibly.

This numerical measure of the Lab's popularity should tell us something else as well. A lot of people are enjoying these dogs for reasons that have nothing to do with the contents of game vests at the end of the day. In fact, it is the Lab's personality rather than the ability to fetch ducks from ice-choked water that has made such a broad cross-section of dog fanciers take notice. And it is my contention that training a versatile retriever is the best way to bring those personality traits into focus, and to enjoy a rewarding relationship with one's dog in the process.

Whatever the breed or level of ability, our dogs are not sterile hunting machines. They are friends and companions that enter our lives fully prepared to enrich them. Ideally, training them to hunt with us should encourage rather than suppress this element of the relationship between man and dog, a process that reaches its fullest development in the training of the versatile retriever.

It is five o'clock on a blustery March morning as I finish this chapter. March is now just about the only month of the year in which I cannot hunt something, which makes it a fine season to rise early and tackle deadlines. After all, it certainly would be nice to finish this manuscript before turkey season.

There is another reason I am awake and at the keyboard already this morning. Last night, by accident, I let Sonny out of the house just as Nick released Becca, our year-old female, from her kennel in the barn. The two of them took off together, as they inevitably do when they are running free outside at the same time, and I spent all night worrying about them despite firm instructions to myself to the contrary.

Finally, after a night of tossing and turning, I gave up, rose in the dark, and went to work. Just as I finished the sentence about dogs entering our lives fully prepared to enrich them, Sonny and Becca finally showed up at the door, covered with mud and smelling of skunk, which serves to remind me that the trainer's work is never truly finished.

It's good to see them anyway.

Choosing Your Weapon

Getting to know someone is a complicated business. For most of us it is a prolonged process, aided immeasurably by time spent in the field where one can observe how prospective friends treat their hunting partners and their dogs. If time is of the essence, a backcountry excursion or a hunt for dangerous game should answer most of the important questions in short order. A week or so of that kind of thing and you will either be friends for life or unable to stand one another's company.

Such time-honored means of evaluating potential outdoor companions are not always practical, however, in which case one must rely on instinct. While my own first impressions are generally accurate enough to prevent major errors in judgment, I like to supplement those impressions with two brief exercises in detection. Given the opportunity to do so without offense, I find it useful to examine a new acquaintance's bookshelves and gun cabinet, because learning what someone reads and shoots often provides ready insight into character.

The contents of my own library are irrelevant here, but for readers who have come this far, it only seems fair to begin a discussion of shotguns with an examination of my own. Excluding the kids' .410s and 20-gauges, I own only four, which is really a meager number for someone who spends as much time in the field as I do. I pointed this out repeatedly to two ex-wives, neither of whom seemed impressed by my deprivation, which may in turn have a direct bearing on my marital status at the time of this writing.

The first, I call the Mud Gun. A perfectly functional 12-gauge pump whose manufacturer I will not embarrass in public, it sports a pistol grip and barely legal barrel that make it look like a prosecution exhibit from a liquor store robbery. All its metal surfaces are pitted and corroded, reflecting the Mud Gun's record as a survivor. While I don't believe in abusing shotguns, this one has been called on to go where no gun has gone before.

The fact is that I do a lot of things in the outdoors besides traditional wingshooting, that call for the presence of a shotgun such as bowhunting dangerous game and taking extended wilderness trips through bear country. Conditions during these undertakings are often miserable, involving rain, condensation, and even saltwater, the source of most of the Mud Gun's worst battle scars. Furthermore, crossing borders into developing countries always raises the possibility that a shotgun will disappear courtesy of some corrupt official. All these factors add up to an argument for owning one shotgun that is expendable, if not downright disposable. When all is going to hell around you, it's no time to worry about the finish on your best double.

I've even shot some birds with the Mud Gun, although a pistol grip does not make for a particularly enjoyable day of wingshooting. Most of the birds so taken have been ptarmigan that would not hold for the bow, and I invariably shot them because I wanted to eat them very badly. Those who hold to the function-is-beauty school of design should find little to fault about the Mud Gun's performance in circumstances such as this.

I have never had to use the Mud Gun for defense, although when its magazine is stacked with alternating loads of slugs and buckshot, it is certainly a formidable tool for that purpose. While it has never fired a shot in anger, it has been a welcome companion on the trail of more than one wounded bear, and I always sleep better in grizzly country knowing that it is there beside me in the tent. One day it will fall over the side of a boat or overdose on saltwater spray and be gone, and when that happens, I shall miss it.

The second of my shotguns looks a bit more respectable in polite society. A 12-gauge Browning over-and-under, it sports thirty-inch barrels, a high, straight stock, and a gross weight guaranteed to make anyone's arms sag after half a day in the field. It began life as a full-and-full, but the manufacturer's tight chokes made that option too much of a good thing, so I opened up the lower barrel and expanded the chambers to accommodate three-inch shells, and now it looks as if it should do just what it is supposed to do, at least on paper.

What it is supposed to do is kill geese and turkeys. I acquired the gun in one of those complex three-way trades in which it is sometimes difficult to keep track of one's original intentions, but there is no doubt that I had pretty much what I wanted when it was all over. The trouble is, the gun is just too big and heavy. It did fine on turkeys, although I did watch one ordinarily dead-eyed Nobel laureate use it to send two shots in a row over the head of a strutting tom at embarrassingly close range. The gun has never felt right in the goose blind despite its specifications, and since

I do all my turkey hunting with a bow nowadays, the big gun just sits in the cabinet, where it's nice to look at while it appreciates in value, which it does at least as well as the stock market.

The third gun contributes a real touch of class to its surroundings. A Parker DHE, it also came to me by way of a trade. I was relieving the gun cabinet of some rifles that I never used anymore, and I'm sure that the trade itself left both parties delighted and certain that they had snookered the other shamelessly, which in a way defines the function of commerce. I probably never would have gone right out and bought a Parker, in which case I never would have known what I was missing.

I take a perverse delight in my own ignorance of both the history and the technical specifications of this gun. I've listened to my share of discussions by true enthusiasts, most of whom would rather talk about guns than talk about dogs or hunting, which immediately establishes a certain cultural distance between us. I just don't care all that much about those things.

Which is not to deny that there many wonderful things about a Parker, most of which I can begin to appreciate as soon as I pick this one up. The gun's balance and linear grace are unique. Since I was not brought up shooting in the side-by-side tradition, the broad sight picture still seems a bit unfamiliar and I may never adjust fully to the second trigger. Nonetheless, the gun feels at home in my hands and when I carry it across the prairie, it evokes its own sense of history. I don't quite know what I would do with a gun like this in tight cover, but here in the wide open spaces, it feels like a natural.

That brings us to gun number four: another Browning 12-gauge over-and-under with twenty-six-inch barrels and improved cylinder and modified choke. I know it doesn't sound well suited to hunting the open country of the plains. Unlike the others, it came to me new in the box, as a gift from my father when I graduated from medical school. Its newness actually put me off a bit at first. It didn't feel or smell quite like the other shotguns of the same manufacture that I learned to shoot as a kid. It's perfectly familiar by now, of course, and I also have the satisfaction of knowing that every bit of wear on the graying metal and every ding on the stock came courtesy of my own hands.

When I ask one of the kids to go down to the gun cabinet and get me my shotgun, this is the one that they return with, no questions asked. Of course, there are reasons for my unabashed attachment to what is really nothing more than a simple construction of wood and steel. Part of this has to do with the gun's function as an enduring gift from the man who taught me to hunt and shoot. My attachment to this gun depends heavily upon my own personal history as well. This is the shotgun I brought with me to the plains in the early 1970s. There followed a decade of unprecedented bounty, during which good habitat conditions, hospitable landowners, generous limits, and my own youthful enthusiasm allowed wingshooting the likes of which few of us will ever experience again. Since I did it all with one dog and one gun, both assumed a special stature among my formative life experiences.

The good ones always do.

M y attitude toward the technical aspects of shotgun performance has been hopelessly biased by my attitude toward gun writers. It's not that I really have anything against them. Several of them are friends, and they even frequent my house, where they have been known to enjoy good food, strong drink, and other elements of hospitality, especially during hunting season. I might not be ready to have my daughter marry one, but I am willing to keep an open mind.

The nonsense that they write is another matter. Patterning your gun. Choosing the optimal load for pheasants. Improved cylinder versus modified. Good grief. The best thing that can be said for these endless theoretical discussions is that they spare gun writers the indignity of having to seek gainful employment. The simple fact of the matter is that truly good shots will shoot well in the field with virtually anything.

This principle was impressed upon me at an early age. An old reformed market hunter who I'll call Pat used to frequent our local skeet club when I was a kid. Pat was well into his 80s I would imagine, an engaging personality, a skilled raconteur, and an absolutely marvelous wingshot despite his advanced age and deteriorating health. And yes, he could turn clay birds to dust with anything.

Pat used to supplement his retirement income by dealing in shotguns. His favorite marketing technique was to lie in wait while some well-heeled visitor embarrassed himself on the skeet range. He would then unobtrusively observe that a shotgun with a tad more drop at heel might be just what was needed. Then he would miraculously produce just such a gun and put on a brief shooting clinic with it. Flush with confidence after this remarkable display of geriatric marksmanship, the visitor would usually proceed to shoot the gun just fine when Pat offered it to him on trial. When product is presented as irresistibly as that, commerce becomes inevitable.

Of course, we regulars knew two things that the proud owner of the new shotgun did not. The first was that the "features" of the new gun were strictly a function of what Pat happened to have available for sale. The second was that despite looking ready for the grave, Pat could put on one of his shooting displays with absolutely any shotgun ever made.

I have observed a great many shooters of varying levels of ability since then. Some are born with the ability to perform this marvelous exercise in hand-eye coordination while others must struggle, sometimes in prolonged frustration. Whatever the case, I remain convinced that shots at flying birds are almost invariably made or missed on the basis of the shooter's ability rather than the specifications of the gun.

Is this an argument in favor of giving up on fine guns and committing ourselves to a lifetime of shooting with whatever comes off the shelf at the hardware store? Of course not. It is an argument in favor of intellectual honesty. I simply suggest that we stop fretting over arcane distinctions among shotguns and get on with the business of hunting with them.

Of course there are legitimate differences between Purdeys and all those generic Mud Guns; it's just that those differences have remarkably little to do with hitting or missing gamebirds on the wing. We should all stop pretending otherwise (unless, of course, some pathetic plea is necessary to convince one's significant other that life without a new fowling piece would be intolerable). Herein lies the real thesis of this chapter: We should enjoy good guns not because we will hit more with them, but because they intrinsically warrant our enjoyment. Admitting as much should enhance our appreciation of the guns we love to love.

The development of true personal affection between man and machine is a quirky business. Cynics should have a field day exploring the alleged psychology by which people become emotionally attached to what are, after all, merely tools. And yet we all know that it happens, and those of us who have experienced the phenomenon invariably come away with the sense that our lives have been made more enjoyable in the process.

In addition to shotguns, I have grown personally attached to two other types of inanimate objects in my life: Super Cubs and longbows. Analysis reveals several characteristics shared by these apparently unrelated objects. All are employed in the accomplishment of difficult tasks. These tasks require intense physical coordination between the device and the person using it. These undertakings sometimes involve an element of danger and often take place in isolated settings without the benefit of human companionship. There are always characteristics sufficient to identify the device in question as unique and to distinguish it from others of its kind, whether that flavor of individuality arises from the selection of woods for the riser of a bow, the arrangement of instruments on an airplane's panel, or the pattern of wear on the stock of a shotgun.

For Americans, firearms fulfill these criteria in a culturally unique way. Historically, guns remained important to individual Americans long after they had been reduced to toys or matters of military necessity elsewhere. Gunsmithing was among the first triumphs of Yankee enterprise. The prolonged existence of a New World frontier allowed our ancestors ample opportunity to come to terms with their weapons under just the sort of isolated, demanding conditions outlined earlier. While such matters of historical fact tend to be reduced to cliché in these days of contentious Second Amendment debate, it is little wonder that American wingshooters tend to go on about their shotguns more than they really need to in order to put pheasants on the table.

I have no real argument with this. While my own gun cabinet is scarcely pretentious, it contains more than anyone really needs, an admission I can make now that I no longer have to defend it against skeptics in my own household. Consider the Parker, for example. Its elegance is apparent even to unsophisticated shooters and those who do not shoot at all. Carried off across the prairie, the gun acts as a magic totem, capable of transporting its bearer back to another, simpler time. The feel of the gun and the companionship of the dog and the wildness of the country sometimes seem to conspire when I am alone out there, and together they make it possible to forget for a while the burdens of our civilization and its discontents.

And that, finally, is why we should care about the guns we carry with us in the field above and beyond their simple ability to enable the harvest of game. At the risk of offense to my friends who manage to write sensibly about chokes and barrel lengths, I would suggest a moratorium on such technical matters, at least here in the company of friends. Let us admit what we already know: We acquire more guns than we need, not because doing so will help us hit more and miss less, but because we enjoy their company. The theoretical union of function and beauty can reach no fuller expression.

Yellow Dog

There aren't a lot of rules in the business of outdoor writing, but here are two of them: Don't write about dead friends or dead dogs. Having willfully violated the first of these tenets, I see no reason to treat the second as inviolate.

The arrival of Skykomish Sunka Zee into our lives came heavily flavored with circumstance. My wife Susan and I were back in Seattle visiting our families one winter when Dick and Ray called from Montana to tell us that our Lab had been struck by a car and killed. The news was devastating. Never mind that the deceased had been a hard-headed, ill-mannered, pain-in-the-ass by all objective criteria. We had no kids then and our dog occupied the affection receptors in the emotional part of the brain ordinarily reserved for one's own children.

By unstated agreement, Dick, Ray, and I have never discussed the details of that dog's death, although I inferred that one of them was at the wheel of the lethal vehicle. After watching me endure several seasons of apoplexy at the hands of the dog, it is even possible that they took advantage of my absence to do me one of the biggest favors of my life. Twenty years after the fact, I don't know and I don't want to know.

But there I was, stranded in Seattle with no hunting dog in my life for the first time ever. My father offered his sympathy (while, I now suspect, he secretly rejoiced in the knowledge that he would not have to hunt with that dog again the following season).

Then he gave me some simple advice: Go find another one. So we did.

There are many theories governing the selection of puppies, most emphasizing a careful analysis of papers and scrutiny of the sire and dam. We didn't have time for any of that. After answering a couple of ads in the paper, we drove out to a farm on the edge of the city and talked to the owners of what sounded like the most promising litter. They impressed me as good people. The dog's papers were in order. With no further ado, I reached down into the wriggling mass of yellow puppies and, in one of the great triumphs of dumb luck, withdrew, at random, what turned out to be the best hunting dog I have ever trained.

We had taken to naming our dogs after our favorite steelhead streams and decided at first to call this one Skykomish Sunrise, after both the river and the steelhead pattern that originated there. Evidently, another enthusiast of steelhead and Labrador retrievers had thought of the same thing, because the AKC bounced that one right back at us. We were living on the Fort Peck Reservation at the time, and while my spoken Sioux was scarcely adequate to find trouble on Saturday night, an elderly Indian friend was able to help me with the translation of yellow dog, and the puppy became Skykomish Sunka Zee.

We lived a long way from the distractions of clear-water trout streams then, and the growing dog enjoyed plenty of attention that summer. By the time bird season approached, it was apparent that Sky was highly precocious. He marked and handled and hunted with plenty of puppy enthusiasm, but remarkably little puppy silliness. The obvious question became: What to do with this developing prodigy come September?

The dog would be nine-months old when bird season opened. There is plenty of opportunity to ruin a dog that age by exposing him to the noise and confusion of the hunt before he is emotionally mature enough for the experience. All young dogs do things in the field that need to be discouraged. If the dog associates the discouragement with the hunt itself rather than the specific infraction, potential may be lost forever. On the other hand, the best students always deserve to be challenged, whether they are adolescent dogs or adolescent children. I tried not to let myself be influenced too much by the fact that nine-month old Sky was now the only dog I had, and that the thought of spending an autumn in eastern Montana without a bird dog was nearly unbearable. That was my problem, I told myself, and I had no business compromising a good young dog just because I needed to go hunting.

Then opening day rolled around at last, and I took him hunting anyway. In retrospect, the decision makes me look like a dog training genius.

On the morning of the first Saturday in September, Dick and I walked down into a grassy swale somewhere in the middle of the prairie with Sky and Dick's setter bouncing along happily in front of us. Several hundred yards later, I crested a little rise to find Sky locked solidly on point in front of me. The sight of a Labrador retriever frozen into a comical parody of a pointing dog stopped me squarely in my tracks.

"You're not going to believe this!" I yelled over to Dick, and when he walked across the draw to join us, he confirmed that he did not. Finally, we recovered from the apparent absurdity of the situation long enough to walk in and flush the covey of sage hens and drop three or four of them, at which point the dog was free to be a retriever once more.

This is not going to be a story about pointing Labs, although legitimate interest in the possibility has now developed in certain retriever breeding circles. For the rest of his career, Sky repeated this performance just often enough to let me know that it was no accident. He pointed once or twice a year for reasons that were never clear or predictable, and when he did, he seemed to do so passively, as if the point was a phenomenon totally beyond his control that left him every bit as mystified as it left us. If that first, glorious demonstration really meant anything more than a few dead birds, it was simply that hunting with Skykomish Sunka Zee was never likely to be boring, and sure enough, it never was.

We enjoyed quite a rookie season together. At first, I promised myself we would stick to sharptails and sage hens because they are easy on young dogs and their pursuit minimizes the need for discipline. As waterfowl season approached, however, it was obvious that the dog was ready for ducks, since he took to the water like an otter. By the time we left the blind on opening day, he had proven himself. Pheasant hunting is the graduate school of dog work for the versatile retriever, but by the end of October I sensed that he was ready. The high plains ringnecks certainly taught him a lesson or two, but he took his lumps in sporting fashion and brought enough of them to hand to establish both his confidence in himself and my own confidence in him.

It was his second season, however, that confirmed the fact that we were beyond the fast-learner category and into the realm of the exceptional.

During the first week of October, we were hunting sharptails and Huns in a broad expanse of prairie surrounding a shallow, manmade lake. The entire lake has since gone dry, but at the time it was one of the largest bodies of water around, measuring several miles across. It usually contained plenty of waterfowl, but there was almost no cover around its edges, and most of the ducks would raft up in the middle where they were all but impossible to hunt.

A broad earthen dam rimmed the western edge of the lake, and as I walked back toward the truck, I decided to climb over the top just to see what was there. As luck would have it, a flock of teal was resting right

behind the dam. It was a long shot from the top of the dam to the waterline, but as the teal flushed, I swung on the nearest bird and broke the tip
of its wing.

The teal splashed back down into the water and began to swim. The
surface of the lake was calm and the dog marked the fall easily. When I
released him from my side, he hit the water with a great geyser of spray
and I settled down in the sagebrush to watch the show.

Puddle ducks with broken wingtips usually lower their profiles and
swim for cover onshore, where their instincts tell them they have the best
chance of eluding their pursuers. Perhaps this bird knew enough to dis-
trust the barren shoreline, for it headed straight toward the middle of the
lake with the dog paddling furiously behind. Teal are surprisingly strong
swimmers, and with the substantial headstart that the long shot provided,
it was apparent that Sky had an epic retrieve in front of him.

I considered whistling the dog back, but losing a cripple is enough to
ruin any day and calling an enthusiastic retriever off a retrieve seems like
a violation of natural order. As the gap between the teal and the dog started to close relentlessly, the duck began to dive. They were several hundred yards from shore by this time, and I assumed that Sky would eventually lose the trail out there in the open water and return to shore. Little
did I know.

It was a bright, sunny afternoon and the surface of the lake shimmered
like a mirage in the distance. I soon lost sight of the bird entirely, and
then the dog's head got smaller and smaller as he circled farther away
across the water, and finally I lost sight of him as well. Few places on
earth feel quite as empty as a calm, flat lake in the middle of the prairie,
especially when it has consumed your favorite hunting dog. As ridiculous
as the situation felt, there was really nothing to do but wait, and so I waited. For an hour and a half, by the watch.

Shadows were lengthening behind the dam by the time a tiny dot
appeared upon the lake's indistinct horizon. It is always hard to tell about
small, distant objects across large reaches of open water. Study the sea
long enough and you can imagine all kinds of things out there. Every
time I do it, I appreciate why whaling captains sent their very best eyes
aloft to the crow's nest. After staring intently and looking away and staring once again, I convinced myself that the object was more than the
product of wishful thinking, that it was getting steadily larger, and finally,
that it really was my dog returning to port at last.

I stood and whistled and waved my arms to give him a point of reference against the background of light in the western sky. The whistle's trill rolled away across the water and then I could hear the dog's swimming noise answer me, a high-pitched sound like a goldeneye in flight that in the years to come would define his enthusiasm for water retrieves. Finally, he got some ground beneath his feet and bounded up out of the water. We met halfway between the dam and the waterline. The teal was resting quietly in his mouth with its dark eye still alert and its plumage unruffled, as if it had merely hitched a ride across the lake.

That was the moment I realized that the next years of my life were going to be special, just as the parents of a musical prodigy or a potential Olympic athlete eventually realize that without really intending to do so, they have become involved in something that may be far larger than themselves.

R ay and I were standing in a blind next to a prairie pothole later that season when we got our first look at another of Sky's unique abilities. Once again, it was not immediately clear that he was going to survive the strength of his own character.

A set of mallards had come into the decoys and we both doubled easily. Three of the birds were stone dead and Sky and Ray's Chessie had them in our hands in short order. The fourth bird was a problem. It had only sustained a broken wing, and nothing challenges a dog quite like a mature mallard with everything still working except its flight apparatus.

I suppose that there are complex rules of engagement that are supposed to apply to these situations, but our own rules are simple: We want our cripples in our hands as quickly and cleanly as possible, and it doesn't matter what dog gets the job done.

I had kept my eye on the last duck, which was heading for the opposite shore in its stealth mode, with nothing but its snout visible above the water. We lined out both dogs and sent them. After a minute or so of pursuit, they had the bird surrounded. Then the mallard sounded, as wounded mallards predictably will. Unable to see or smell the submerged duck, Ray's Chessie thrashed about the water frantically. Sky, on the other hand, dove right along with the bird.

At first we assumed that he had simply ducked underwater in an attempt to grab the mallard as it swam past him, but he failed to surface.

The Chessie steamed in circles. Ray expressed his bewilderment. I began to fret, imagining all sorts of underwater mishaps that might befall a dog. Finally a boil appeared on the brown water like a whale breaching and there was Sky, a good twenty yards from the spot where he had disappeared. And yes, he had the mallard held firmly but gently in his mouth.

Years later, I learned of a professional trainer who deliberately tried to teach retrievers to dive in the pursuit of swimming ducks.

He used an elaborate system of pulleys to draw training dummies progressively deeper under water, and claimed some success in getting his dogs to perform this spectacular maneuver. Based on years of experience with Sky, I can only say that the end result is well worth some effort if you appreciate dramatic retrieves, and that it's a hell of a lot easier to get the job done if you start with a dog who knows the trick in the first place.

The underwater retrieve became one of Sky's signature techniques, and he performed it with such mastery that I always wished we could name it for him somehow, like a Sukahara on the rings or an Immelmann in the air. It was not just a matter of putting his head underwater to take a swipe at a duck as if he were bobbing for apples. He went down, like a submarine, and when something had to come up for air, it was almost always the duck. First time observers invariably gasped as the seconds ticked by, while those of us who knew Sky waited patiently, confident that something amazing was in progress right before our eyes.

I had two more years of medical training to get out of the way, so Sky spent his third and fourth seasons in Seattle rather than the bird-rich environment of the Montana prairie. All was not lost, however. The University of Washington was developing rural medical training programs around the Northwest, and, protesting like B'rer Rabbit on the edge of the briar patch, I volunteered to spend both autumns of my internal medicine residency back in Montana on assignments no one else wanted. It was a tough job, but someone had to do it. And once we were back in the bird cover, Sky acted as if we had never left.

I returned to eastern Montana as soon as possible, and during the years that followed, Sky performed at his absolute prime. In the late 70s, the drought had not yet impacted prairie duck populations and Hun and sharptail numbers were at their peak. It is difficult to imagine that any dog in America had more wild birds of more different species shot over him than Sky did during that period of time. He was still young enough to hunt all day, but experienced enough to know what he was doing, and I suppose the same can be said for those of us who hunted with him. Ray handled some good Chessies then, and an amicable inter-service rivalry developed between us on behalf of our dogs, culminating in the nearly mystical tradition of the Retrieve of the Year honor. No matter how dramatic the Chessies' water entries or how stalwart they were in the face of cold, Sky always managed to do something so amazing that the Retrieve of the Year became his personal province. Chesapeake Bay retriever chauvinist that he was and always will be, even Ray had to admit that Sky was the dog of a lifetime.

Of course, even the greatest dogs have their faults and Sky was no exception. In fact, he had two peculiar habits that threatened to drive me crazy until I learned to put them both in perspective.

The first was a tendency to become psychotic under high wind conditions. One day early in his second season, we were walking back to our truck in a real prairie howler. A covey of Huns rose at the edge of a stubble field and I somehow managed to double in spite of the gale. Both birds were stone dead in the open, forty yards upwind of us, and it looked like an absolutely routine retrieve. Halfway to the birds, the dog stopped with the air breaking around him like water in a trout stream, and refused to advance farther. He tacked back and forth across the swirling current with his nose held high, trying to decipher the torrent of scent. He just couldn't do it. His guidance systems had come undone. I watched him work back and forth aimlessly for ten or fifteen minutes before I walked out into the stubble and showed him the birds. Even then, he acted as if he didn't believe they were real.

We watched him repeat that performance once or twice each season, always when working into brisk, swirling wind. Lots of dogs have difficulty under such conditions, but they reduced Sky to utter helplessness. I think that his nose was just so good that he didn't know what to do when it misled him.

His second fault was even stranger. Despite having one of the softest mouths of any dog I have ever hunted with, Sky could not let a season pass without eating one bird.

And I do mean eat. I never saw him romp with a bird, or hard mouth one. Of the untold number of birds and ducks that he retrieved for me over the years, I cannot remember one arriving at hand with a puncture wound courtesy of the dog. But once a season he would select a bird at random from the vast number at his disposal and devour it.

These transgressions never seemed to correlate with anything. Sometimes it would be a duck, sometimes a grouse, sometimes a pheasant. The dog was always well-fed and the offenses took place under a wide variety of hunting conditions. It seemed to be something that he just could not help doing.

He did it for the first time during his puppy season. I dismissed the offense as youthful indiscretion and, in accordance with my promises to myself, I didn't come down on him too hard. When he repeated the same crime during his derby year, however, he obviously knew better, as confirmed by the painfully guilty look on his feather-coated face when I happened upon the scene of the crime. His grace period was over, and I got after him about as hard as I ever got after him for anything. He took his licks bravely and without resentment, as always, and for the rest of the season, he treated the birds in his mouth the way a mother would treat a newborn baby.

It took me two more seasons to accept the fact that he was going to eat a bird now and then no matter what I did, at which point I simply hoped that he would have the courtesy to engage in these misbehaviors when we were alone, rather than in the company of impressionable friends. Of course, it didn't always work out that way. During one of my medical residency years, my father stopped in Billings for a quick weekend of bird hunting. We drove south into unfamiliar country and spent all day hiking through cactus containing some of the biggest rattlesnakes I have ever seen in my life. After hours and hours in the rising heat, we finally jumped a small covey of Huns and he dropped one, at which point we decided to retreat before the snakes ate us. On the way home, we pulled into a cafe to rehydrate and when we came back out, the truck was awash in feathers. Ten man-hours of labor had disappeared into the gullet of a Labrador retriever, at which point there wasn't anything left to do but head for home and a bottle of bourbon to contemplate the meaning of it all.

In time, I gave up and stopped punishing him physically for these once-a-year exercises in delinquency. I always disliked whacking him anyway, and it clearly wasn't doing any good. When I caught him in the act, I would sit him down with as much evidence present as I could muster. Then I would kneel right on the ground in front of him and stare him in the eye until he could not stand the burden of his own sins any longer. Finally, I would get in his face and snarl, *"You shit-head!"* with as much dramatic contempt as I could manage, and when he looked away in misery we would be done with it for the year.

I do not propose this training method as a mater of general principle, but in the end it seemed to work for us.

Sky was seven-years old when we moved to Alaska. We had kids of our own by then (kids without floppy ears and long tails, that is), but the detachment that developed between my kennel and me had nothing to do with sibling competition. Bird hunting in the far north is a bit of a stretch, at least if you are accustomed to the plains of eastern Montana. Alaska is every bowhunter's dream, however, and so for several years I spent most of my free time during hunting season with my longbow in pursuit of sheep and moose and caribou. Sky took all this in stride because he was a gentleman.

He still never failed to display enthusiasm when given a chance, and many of my ptarmigan hunts and ritual trips to the Duck Shack were made largely for his benefit.

November is a grim month in southcentral Alaska, especially for an outdoorsman accustomed to looking forward to November all year long. After a season or two of trying desperately to conjure up some kind of outdoor sport from the cold and dark, I got smart and made a return trip to my Montana roots part of my regular November itinerary. We would stay at Ray's and hunt pheasants in the morning and whitetails in the evening, and no matter how cold it became in our tree stands I sensed that there was no better place on earth to be.

Sky went with me, of course. Transporting a dog through the world's airline system is one of life's great hassles, and one in which, despite the well-known business maxim to the contrary, the customer is always wrong. On every one of those trips, I reached the point of screaming in rage at various airline bean-counters over some stupid rule governing the transport of Labrador retrievers from Alaska to Montana and back, but there really wasn't much to be done about it. I wasn't going to Montana in November without a bird dog, especially that bird dog. Period.

On our third such excursion, we spent the first day hunting pheasants from dawn until dark. The weather had been dry and that was the first of several poor upland bird seasons in a row, but my own legs were full of spring from months of hard hunting in Alaska and it didn't bother anyone that we had to work hard for our birds. Sky looked tired that night and I hand fed him an extra ration of something nutritious. The following morning, he was a bit less bouncy than usual but he still seemed eager to go. We found more birds that day and limited by noon. I put the dog in Ray's kennel to rest up a bit and then we set off to hunt whitetails.

That evening, I went out to feed the dogs and discovered that Sky wouldn't stand up. I could not find anything specific wrong with him, and it took me a long, sleepless night to realize that he wasn't sick at all. There hadn't been enough bird hunting in Alaska to reveal the obvious, but a day and a half on the prairie had left him no room to hide. The simple fact was that he had grown old.

From then on, hunting with Sky was largely a matter of ceremony. We moved back to Montana the following year to stay, and he survived the trip down the highway without ill effect. I took him out a time or two that fall and let him snuffle around in the bird cover, but that was about all he could manage. It was obvious that he had made his last water retrieve and, by the end of the season, it was obvious that he had made his last bird hunt as well.

One tragedy of great dogs is that their very greatness makes it all but impossible to groom their replacements. I had brought several pups along during the years I hunted with Sky, but none of them seemed to show any real promise, perhaps because my own notion of promise had been hopelessly skewed by the dog already waiting to go whenever I wanted to hunt birds. Those pups all wound up as potlickers or kids' dogs or refugees in good country homes.

Perhaps if I had worked a little longer or a little harder with one or two of them...Who knows?

The second tragedy of great dogs is that due to the inner workings of our various biological clocks, we will almost always outlive them. When that happens, you can expect a great emptiness to appear where vitality and enthusiasm once reigned, and that emptiness is never easy to reconcile. That's what happened the first spring after our return from Alaska, when Sky walked out in the yard one day and lay down and died. The fact that each of us can only hope (often in futility) for an equally serene end was little consolation to me at first. I missed my dog, and not just because I would never shoot as many birds without him. I missed him because he defined one segment of my life, and now that chapter was over.

Life does go on, however. With no impossible standard left to compromise the process, I reached into another squirming litter of puppies, closed my eyes, and grabbed. I tried to remember the smell of the barn on the outskirts of Seattle and the way I let my fingers run across all those wriggling bodies, and I tried to do everything the same way, just as a gambler will try to throw the dice the same way he did when he hit the biggest numbers of his life.

Luck prevailed. I picked Sonny. He promises to be another story someday, and I can imagine no more elegant ending to a tale about the dogs that bring meaning to our lives.